Weakening Welfare

Weakening Welfare

The Public Distribution of Food in India

Madhura Swaminathan

LeftWord

Offset edition first published in February 2000
Digital print edition, March 2020

LeftWord Books
2254/2A, Shadi Khampur
New Ranjit Nagar
New Delhi 110008
India

LeftWord Books is a division of
Naya Rasta Publishers Pvt. Ltd.

www.leftword.com

ISBN   978-81-87496-08-3

Contents

Acknowledgements

The research for this monograph was conducted at the Indira Gandhi Institute of Development Research (IGIDR) and at the London School of Economics (LSE), which I visited as a Ratan Tata Fellow. The IGIDR provided excellent institutional support, including library and computer facilities, and it supported my field work in rural Maharashtra as well. The Ratan Tata Fellowship at the Asia Research Centre at the LSE provided me with an opportunity to work without interruption on issues of food security.

Kiran Moghe, Mariam Dhawale and other activists of the Janwadi Mahila Sanghathana helped me with fieldwork and shared their ideas and experiences with me. Officials of the Food Corporation of India and of the Department of Food and Civil Supplies, Ministry of Food and Consumer Affairs, Government of India, were very helpful in response to my requests for information. M.D. Asthana was particularly helpful in providing data and information for my research. Jesim Pais helped prepare the statistical tables and graphs in this monograph. I am very grateful to all of them.

My greatest debt is to V.K. Ramachandran, who has helped this work at every stage of the research and writing.

I have written this monograph for my father, whose life-work has been dedicated to making India food-secure.

Mumbai   MADHURA SWAMINATHAN
January 2000

one

Introduction

The system of public distribution of food – henceforth PDS – in India is sixty years old. Over these sixty years, there have been important changes in the scale and scope of public distribution. Nevertheless, for most of this period, the need for a system of delivery of cheap food was not questioned. In the 1990s, however, under the regime of orthodox economic reform and structural adjustment, the objective of expenditure reduction has taken priority over welfare objectives such as the objective of providing food security. In a country where there is mass poverty, where food consumption is low, where about half the adults and children suffer malnutrition and where expenditure on food accounts for the bulk of total family expenditure, we need to expand and strengthen – and not undermine or disband – effective policies of food security.

The subject matter of this monograph is one aspect of food security, that is, the policy of food distribution as implemented by means of PDS. The research and writing here are motivated mainly by two factors. The first is the continued importance of food security in a land with millions of poor and undernourished persons, and the second is the threat to food security in the current context of liberalization, structural adjustment and the associated weakening of welfare systems.

The evidence on food consumption and nutrition, presented in Chapter 3, establishes that food deprivation and food insecurity persist on a mass scale. A concern for effective policies of food distribution does not, however, constitute a defence of the public distribution system in its present form. There is little doubt that PDS has failed in large parts of the country to provide nutritional support to the people and requires genuine reform. In Chapter 4, the successes and failures of PDS are examined in some detail in order to understand what needs to be done. The analysis shows that the big picture is one of low utilization, limited access to food among the poor, rising prices and large-scale leakage from the system. However, there is one clear exception – the state of Kerala – where coverage of PDS is near-universal, where substantial quantities of cereals are available, where the majority of people have access to fair-price shops and where the delivery system functions without excessive corruption and malpractice.

The weaknesses of the public delivery system have been exacerbated by the introduction of structural adjustment policies in the 1990s. Since India's experiments with structural adjustment are relatively recent, I briefly review the international experience, specifically the experience of Mexico, Sri Lanka, Jamaica, Zambia and Tunisia, to identify the impact of structural adjustment on food subsidies, and on the consumption, nutrition and food security of vulnerable populations (Chapter 5). These experiences show that policies of structural adjustment have worsened economic and social inequalities and imposed further hardship on the poor.

I then turn to the policy changes introduced in India since 1991 (Chapter 6). The period of liberalization has seen a further weakening of PDS. The diminished commitment to PDS is reflected in changes in policy, in the inflation in food prices, in the decline in quantities supplied to the distribution network and, most recently, in the introduction of targeting. Targeting food supply in PDS to a narrow section of the population is a dangerous policy, and a prelude to closing down PDS altogether. Targeting is not costless with respect to the welfare of the people; the vast literature on the costs of targeting is summarized in an Appendix to Chapter 6.

If we are not to allow the already inadequate and piecemeal system of food security in India, and this includes the system of public distribution of food, to be weakened further, what needs to be done? How should PDS be strengthened and made an effective means of providing food security for the masses of poor and undernourished people? Chapter 7 presents a set of proposals for a genuine reform of PDS. A summary of the main arguments is set out in Chapter 8.

Structural adjustment and food security

The debate on food subsidies has taken a new turn with the introduction of programmes of orthodox stabilization and structural adjustment. Typically a stabilization package comprises policies for expenditure reduction (to control the fiscal deficit) and expenditure 'switching' (to control the balance of payments or external deficit). These changes in expenditure are brought about by policies of devaluation, monetary tightening (such as through changes in interest rates) and fiscal contraction. Structural adjustment entails a wider set of policies to restructure different sectors of the economy and includes changes in trade, in the orientation of agriculture, and in the role of public and private sector in the economy. Lance Taylor identified the following components of a typical structural adjustment programme: liberalized trade, fiscal restructuring, increasing public sector 'efficiency', financial sector reform and specific programmes in the agriculture, industry, transport and energy sectors (Taylor 1991). Proponents of orthodox policies assume that the goal of higher economic growth can be achieved 'by first "stabilizing" the macro-economy . . . followed by "adjusting" the market through supply side reforms' (Taylor and Pieper 1996: 1).

What are the implications of structural adjustment for food security? Programmes of structural adjustment affect both availability of food at the national level and food security at the household level (FAO 1989). There are four types of effects on food policy:

1. With a shift in strategy towards a more export-oriented economy, patterns of production in the agricultural sector are likely to change and food production for the domestic economy to be affected. To put it differently, the goal of self-sufficiency in production is relinquished in favour of production for export and integration into world trade.

2. Devaluation and other macroeconomic changes affect the absolute and relative price of food commodities as well as food price inflation.

3. Changes in the pattern of public expenditure by governments affect food subsidies and expenditure on agriculture through changes in input subsidies, public investment, and so on.
4. Economy-wide changes in poverty, in inequality and in unemployment are all likely to affect real incomes and household food security.

Let me elaborate on each of these factors, in reverse order. There is now a large body of evidence showing that stabilization and structural adjustment programmes have negative effects on poverty and inequality. 'Besides slowing growth', they tend to make 'income distribution concentrated, increase poverty and reduce social well-being' (Taylor and Pieper 1996: 2). The recent economic history of the less-developed world makes it quite clear that structural adjustment and the accompanying liberalization of less-developed economies have worsened the economic and social condition of vast sections of the population in the affected economies. The shifts in real income and wages brought about by deflationary policies have implications for food consumption and nutrition. The impact of changes in incomes is particularly acute for households in which food is the single largest item of the family budget.

A primary objective of stabilization policy is to reduce the fiscal deficit; the main route envisaged for this is a reduction in public expenditure. Although there are many aspects to public expenditure reform, cutbacks in subsidies are the most widely advocated means of 'reform'. Specifically, a reduction in food subsidies has been one of the most controversial components of programmes of structural adjustment (Taylor 1988: 21). In India too, the rhetoric of cutting down subsidies has been very strong in the period after 1991, and major changes in food policy have been motivated primarily by the goal of expenditure reduction (Chapter 6). While a reduction in subsidies is seen as a major objective of policy, the counterpart of enhancing revenues, especially tax revenues, is given much less weight.

In addition to a reduction in explicit food subsidies, structural adjustment usually entails a reduction in implicit food subsidies, the most obvious outcome of which is food price inflation. Devaluation, for example, raises the price of imported commodities including food and has been accompanied by sharp increases in food prices in many countries. Sharp increases in food prices during periods of structural adjustment have often led to mass protests and riots (Watton and Seddon 1994).

Lastly, emphasis on export orientation in production alters cropping patterns and domestic production becomes dependent on patterns of international demand and changes in international markets. It has been argued that, given fixed resources, mainly land, an inverse relation is likely between export production and production for domestic consumption (Patnaik 1996). If land use changes in the direction of greater allocation of land for export crops, then the allocation of land for food crops required for domestic consumption is likely to fall. The impact on domestic food supply depends, then, on the extent of growth in productivity.[1] In many countries, a shift in production in favour of export crops has been accompanied by a fall in production of grains for domestic consumption and an increase in dependence on imports to meet domestic food requirements. Mexico is a good example. After the end of the SAM (Mexican Food System or Sistema Alimentario Mexicano) programme, there was a cut-back in agricultural subsidies, domestic food production stagnated and Mexico imported about three times as much corn in the 1980s as it did in the 1970s.[2] The programme of liberalization in the 1980s and 1990s eroded the objective of self-sufficiency in food production and domestic consumers of food grain in Mexico are now vulnerable to changes in international markets and prices (Appendini 1997).

Although I have attempted to keep the presentation and discussion of the analysis in this monograph non-technical, there is a concluding section to each chapter that attempts to highlight, without detailed discussion of the data, the main findings of the chapter. While PDS supplies many commodities, the focus of this monograph in on food grain, specifically, rice and wheat.

---

[1] In India, for example, although there has been a reduction in cultivated area under cereal crops in recent years, this has been not been accompanied by a fall in the production of cereals. The output of rice and wheat has continued to increase due to growth in productivity, particularly in erstwhile less productive regions. There has, however, been stagnation in the production of cereals other than rice and wheat.

[2] Mexico imported 26 million tonnes of food in 1970–79 and 60 million tonnes in 1981–88 (Brachet-Marquez and Sherraden, 1994).

two

PDS in India

Phases of Development

There are four major forms of intervention by government in food grain markets in India. First, there is a system of public procurement of food grain. Secondly, the state manages food stocks through storage and buffer-stock operations. Thirdly, there is a state-guided system of delivery of cheap food, the public distribution system (PDS). Fourthly, the government intervenes in trade, and there are legal controls on hoarding and other aspects of internal trade and restrictions on external trade. Direct interventions in procurement and distribution are undertaken by the Food Corporation of India (FCI).

The public distribution system

Objectives
From its inception, the objectives of PDS have included the following:

- rationing during situations of scarcity,
- maintaining price stability,
- keeping a check on private trade, and
- raising the welfare of the poor (by providing basic foods to the vulnerable population at reasonable prices) (Bapna 1990).

The emphasis on different objectives has, of course, changed over time. In Chapter 4, we examine the working of PDS, and assess its functioning in relation to these objectives.

Structure and working of PDS

The organizational structure of PDS is depicted in Figure 2.1 (overleaf). The Department of Food and Civil Supplies, in the Ministry of Food, has the primary responsibility for policies of food procurement and food distribution through PDS. The Food Corporation of India (FCI), set up in 1964 and under the jurisdiction of this department, is the sole central agency in charge of procurement, storage, transport and distribution of food commodities. The FCI is an implementing body and implements the government's policies on procurement, storage, transport and distribution. Often, procurement is undertaken by state co-operative marketing federations and supplied to the FCI. From the FCI, state governments purchase the commodities required for distribution within their states, and the states are, then, responsible for supplying the commodities to fair price shops. Thus, the responsibility for implementing, monitoring and enforcing legal provisions relating to public delivery rests with state governments. The implementing agency at the state level is the state civil supplies department or corporation.

PDS is a rationing mechanism that entitles households to specified quantities of selected commodities at subsidized prices. In most parts of the country, PDS has been universal and all households, rural and urban, with a registered residential address are entitled to rations.[1] Eligible households are given a ration card that entitles them to buy fixed rations (varying with household size and age composition) of selected commodities. The exact entitlement (quantity, range of commodities and prices) varies across states. There have been major changes in entitlements in the last few years, and these are described in Chapter 6.

The six essential commodities supplied through PDS nationally are rice, wheat, sugar, edible oils, kerosene and coal. Additional commodities like pulses, salt, tea are supplied selectively. The commodities are made available through a network of fair-price shops. In 1998, there were a total

---

[1] However, not all households have the same entitlement. In some states, for example, there are dual or triple cards and different types of card-holders have different entitlements.

FIGURE 2.1 *Organizational structure of PDS in India*

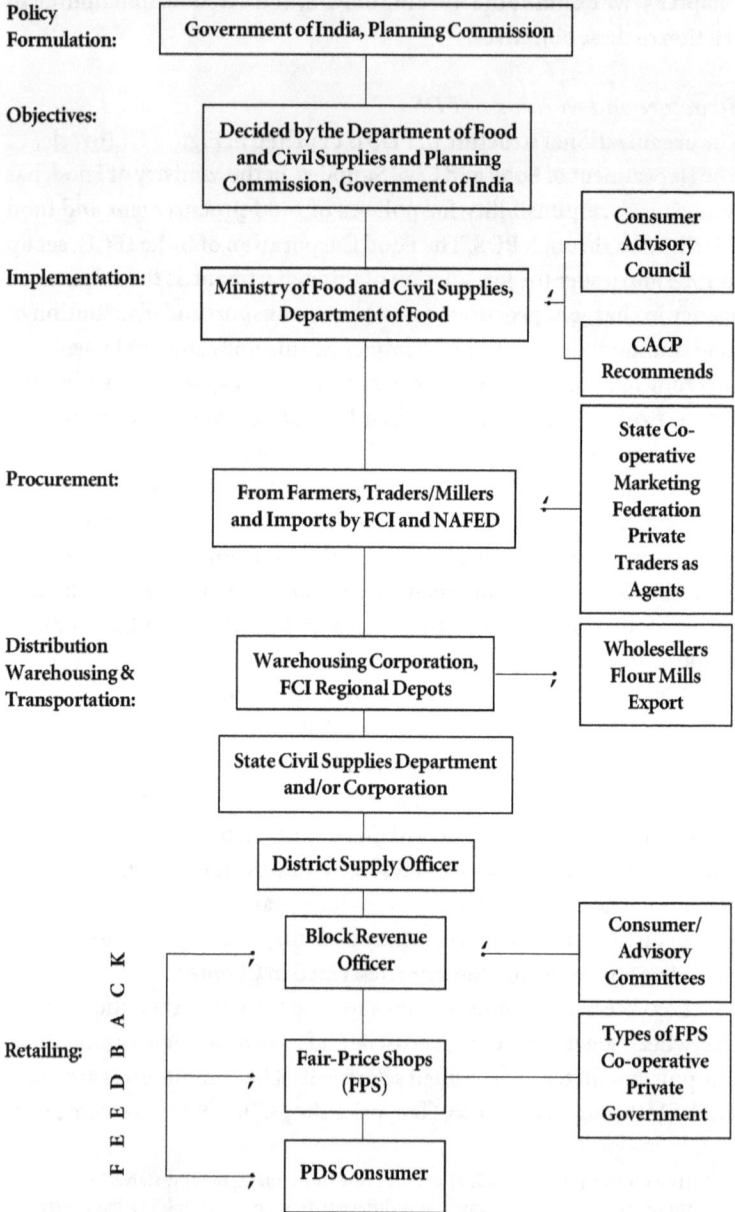

Policy
Formulation:
Government of India, Planning Commission

Objectives:
Decided by the Department of Food
and Civil Supplies and Planning
Commission, Government of India

Consumer
Advisory
Council

Implementation:
Ministry of Food and Civil Supplies,
Department of Food

CACP
Recommends

State Co-
operative
Marketing
Federation
Private
Traders as
Agents

Procurement:
From Farmers, Traders/Millers
and Imports by FCI and NAFED

Distribution
Warehousing &
Transportation:
Warehousing Corporation,
FCI Regional Depots

Wholesellers
Flour Mills
Export

State Civil Supplies Department
and/or Corporation

District Supply Officer

Block Revenue
Officer

Consumer/
Advisory
Committees

Retailing:
FEEDBACK

Fair-Price Shops
(FPS)

Types of FPS
Co-operative
Private
Government

PDS Consumer

Source   Bapna (1990)

of 4.5 lakh fair-price shops in the country, of which 3.6 lakh were in rural areas. These shops were run by private agents and co-operatives and a few were state-owned. As of 1995, there were a total of 182.8 million families with ration cards in the country and, on average, there were 406 ration cards assigned to each fair price shop.

Origins of PDS and phases of development

Public distribution was first started in 1939 as a war-time rationing measure. The British government introduced it in Bombay and later extended it to six other cities and a few regions. The drought and food shortages of the mid-sixties highlighted the need for strengthening and continuing with a system of food distribution and PDS was made a universal scheme in the 1970s. S.L. Bapna (1990) has a useful classification of the evolution of PDS in terms of three phases and I have added the fourth and last phase. Table 2.1 (overleaf) records the net production, imports, net availability, procurement and public distribution of food grain from 1951 to 1998, and a glance at this Table makes the demarcation of these four phases clearer.

Phase I: Origins to 1960
In response to war-time scarcities, the British government introduced rationing and several price control measures.[2] The system grew slowly, from the initial seven cities to 13 cities in 1943, 103 cities and towns in 1944 and 771 cities and towns in 1946. The first area where rural rationing was introduced, and this was on account of strong grassroots political demand for rationing, was Malabar (see Chapter 4). Rationing was abolished in 1947, at the recommendation of the Second Foodgrain Policy Committee, but was reintroduced in 1950 as a welfare measure, with the onset of planning. In the 1950s, PDS was extended to certain rural areas (these were mainly areas viewed as food-deficit regions) but the coverage was mainly in urban areas. As Table 2.1 indicates, the amount of food grain distributed through PDS declined during the 1950s and through to the early 1960s. Further, for most of this period, the quantity distributed through PDS was greater than the quantity procured domestically, and

---

[2] I have drawn on Bapna (1990) for a discussion of the first three phases.

TABLE 2.1 *Availability, procurement and public distribution of food grain India, 1951–98 (in million tonnes)*

Year	Net production	Net imports	Net availability (NA)	Procurement	Public distribution (PD)	PD/NA (%)
1951	48.1	4.82	52.4	3.8	8.0	15.3
1952	48.7	3.9	52.0	3.5	6.8	13.1
1953	54.1	2.0	56.6	2.1	4.6	8.1
1954	63.3	0.8	63.9	1.4	2.2	3.4
1955	61.9	0.5	63.2	1.3	1.6	2.5
1956	60.7	1.4	62.6	Neg.	2.1	3.4
1957	63.4	3.6	66.2	0.3	3.1	4.7
1958	58.3	3.2	61.8	0.5	4.0	6.5
1959	69.0	3.9	72.3	1.8	5.2	7.2
1960	67.5	5.1	71.2	1.3	4.9	6.9
1961	72.0	3.5	75.7	0.5	4.0	5.3
1962	72.1	3.6	76.1	0.5	4.4	5.7
1963	70.3	4.5	74.8	0.8	5.2	6.9
1964	70.6	6.2	78.1	1.4	8.7	11.1
1965	78.2	7.4	84.6	4.0	10.1	11.9
1966	63.6	10.3	73.5	4.0	14.1	19.2
1967	65.0	8.7	73.9	4.5	13.2	17.8
1968	83.2	5.7	86.8	6.8	10.2	11.8
1969	82.3	3.8	85.6	6.4	9.4	11.0
1970	87.1	3.6	89.5	6.7	8.8	9.9
1971	94.9	2.0	94.3	8.9	7.8	8.3
1972	92.0	-0.5	96.2	7.7	10.5	10.9
1973	84.9	3.6	88.8	8.4	11.4	12.8
1974	91.6	5.2	97.1	5.6	10.8	11.1
1975	87.4	7.5	89.3	9.6	11.3	12.6

Contd.

PDS thus depended on imports of food grain, primarily under the US Public Law 480 (PL-480) regime.

Phase II: 1960–78

In the 1960s, there were major changes in the organization of food policy in India. In response to crop failures, food shortages, and price fluctuations, it was decided to make PDS a permanent and universal programme. Two new organizations, the Agricultural Prices Commission (later renamed the Commission on Agricultural Costs and Prices or CACP) and the Food Corporation of India were set up in 1965. The droughts of 1965–66 and 1966–67 provided a strong impetus for the expansion of PDS. Food grain distributed in PDS grew to more than 10 million tonnes in 1965. During

TABLE 2.1 *Contd.*

Year	Net production	Net imports	Net availability (NA)	Procurement	Public distribution (PD)	PD/NA (%)
1976	105.9	0.7	95.8	12.8	9.2	9.6
1977	97.3	0.1	99.0	9.9	11.7	11.8
1978	110.6	-0.6	110.2	11.1	10.2	9.2
1979	115.4	-0.2	114.9	13.8	11.7	10.2
1980	96.0	-0.3	101.4	11.2	15.0	14.8
1981	113.4	0.7	114.3	13.0	13.0	11.4
1982	116.6	1.6	116.9	15.4	14.8	12.6
1983	113.3	4.1	114.7	15.6	16.2	14.1
1984	133.3	2.4	128.6	18.7	13.3	10.4
1985	127.4	-0.4	124.3	20.1	15.8	12.7
1986	131.6	0.5	133.8	19.7	17.3	12.9
1987	125.5	-0.2	134.8	15.7	18.7	13.8
1988	122.8	3.8	130.8	14.1	18.6	14.2
1989	148.7	1.2	147.2	18.9	16.4	11.1
1990	149.7	1.3	144.8	24.0	16.0	11.0
1991	154.3	-0.1	158.6	19.6	20.8	13.1
1992	147.3	-0.4	148.4	17.9	18.8	12.7
1993	157.5	3.1	149.8	28.0	16.4	10.9
1994	161.2	1.1	154.8	26.0	14.0	9.1
1995	167.6	0.4	169.8	22.6	15.3	9.0
1996	157.9	-1.2	165.2	19.8	18.3	11.1
1997	174.4	1.0	177.2	23.6	17.5	9.8
1998	169.0	2.0	170.4	25.5	18.4*	10.8

* Information obtained from the Department of Food and Civil Supplies, Ministry of Food and Consumer Affairs.

Source Government of India, *Economic Survey 1998-99*.

the period 1965–68, PDS depended heavily on imports of food (imports peaked at 10 million tonnes in 1966). Gradually, as food production grew, imports fell and purchases from PDS also fell, but after the drought of 1972–73, the distribution of food grain in PDS picked up again.

Phase III: 1978–91

This phase is marked by the growth of comfortable buffer stocks, and this provided the basis for the large-scale expansion of PDS as well as Food-for-Work type employment programmes. From 1978 onwards, there was a steady growth in the quantity of food grain distributed through PDS, with a peak provision of 20.8 million tonnes in 1991. During the late 1970s and 1980s, PDS was viewed as a component of the strategy to alleviate poverty. The network of fair-price shops grew in the 1970s, as did the

number of commodities supplied in these shops. Special schemes were
introduced in states such as Andhra Pradesh to expand the supply of cheap
food to the poor.

Phase IV: 1991 to present

After 1991, the start of the fourth phase, the amount of food grain
distributed through PDS has fallen substantially, from 20.8 million tonnes
in 1991 to 14 million tonnes in 1994. This fall in distribution has been
accompanied by a rise in stocks, and excessive holdings of stocks. One of
the reasons for this fall in purchases from PDS is the narrowing price
differential between PDS and market prices. Although distribution of food
grain through PDS has risen in the last few years, it remains below the
peak of 1991. There have also been major changes in the structure of PDS
in the 1990s, most importantly the introduction of targeting in 1997. The
weakening of PDS in the 1990s and the policy changes that contributed to
it are discussed in Chapter 6.

Variations over time

In addition to the broad phases of growth sketched above, there have, of
course, been important fluctuations in the quantity of grain distributed
from year to year.[3] In years of drought, for example, the supply of grain
from PDS has increased relative to normal years. Between 1970–72, the
ratio of food grain sold in PDS to total net availability was around 10 per
cent but the share of PDS grain in net availability went up to 12 per cent in
1973–74 when several parts of the country faced a drought. In Maharashtra,
where drought conditions were severe for three years in a row, the allocation
of food grain from the centre rose from 17.4 lakh tonnes in 1972 to 23.3
lakh tonnes in 1973 (Subramanian 1975). The number of fair price shops
also grew, from 24,492 in 1969 to 25,295 in 1972 and by another 4,300 in
1973 (ibid.). The expansion of shops was most rapid in the acutely affected
districts. Similarly, during the drought of 1987–88 in Rajasthan, Gujarat
and Madhya Pradesh, there was an expansion in the supply of cheap food
via PDS. According to Tendulkar, Sundaram and Jain (1994) consumption
of cereals rose in 1987–88 in Gujarat and Rajasthan despite a sharp fall in

---

[3] While there are changes in the amount of food grain allocated and purchased through
the PDS from month to month, these variations are rather small and we shall not
discuss them further (see Bhalla 1994).

output because of the contribution of PDS and massive drought relief work.

Summing up

To sum up, PDS grew from a rationing scheme in big cities during the Second World War into a universal programme for the provision of cheap food and a component of the strategy to alleviate poverty. I demarcated four phases in the growth of PDS. In the first phase (1939–60), PDS had a restricted coverage. Major organizational changes were introduced in the second phase (1960–78) and this period saw the gradual expansion of PDS network. In the third phase (1979–91), the growth of domestic production allowed for a sustained expansion of public distribution. The last and current phase is that of the period of structural adjustment, a phase of weakening of the system of public distribution.

three

Why We Need
a System of Food Distribution

Chronic hunger and malnutrition remain widespread in India. Fifty-two years after Independence, the large majority of our population is under-nourished. The incidence of hunger has worsened in recent years in many parts of the country. There are areas as well where deaths by starvation continue to occur. This chapter brings together the available evidence on indicators of poverty, especially indicators of deprivation in food and nutrition, with the objective of creating a picture of the scale and severity of hunger and malnutrition in India today. The indicators that are discussed are:

- income poverty,
- levels of food consumption,
- calorie intake,
- intake of micronutrients,
- nutritional status, and
- food share or share of expenditure on food in total household expenditure.

The two main sources of data on consumption and nutrition in India are the surveys on consumption expenditure conducted by the National Sample Survey (NSS) Organization and the surveys conducted by the National Nutrition Monitoring Bureau (NNMB). The surveys of the NSS have national coverage whereas the NNMB surveys have been undertaken in certain selected states of the country.

Income poverty

When economists and policy-makers speak of the scale of poverty, they usually refer to *income*-poverty and the commonly used measures of income-poverty are the number and proportion of households that are below the official poverty line. The poverty line, in turn, is a measure of the income or expenditure required to purchase a food basket that generates a minimum number of calories. According to the Planning Commission, the required per capita daily intake of calories is around 2,400 in rural areas and 2,100 in urban areas. The official poverty line in India is thus pegged at Rs 49 for rural areas and Rs 57 for urban areas at 1973–74 prices, a very low absolute level of expenditure. At 1993–94 prices, the poverty line is around Rs 206 per capita per month for rural areas and Rs 287 for urban areas.[1] That the income level represented by the poverty line is very meagre is recognized even in official documents. The Perspective Planning Division of the Planning Commission described the norm as 'too meagre to sustain a level of living which would be considered tolerable in the modern context' (cited in Srinivasan and Bardhan 1974: 12).

The first feature of income-poverty in India is that the number of people who are below even the official poverty line is immense. The population of the income-poor in India was 320.5 million in 1993–94.[2] To put that figure in perspective, the number is substantially more than the *combined* population of the Scandinavian countries, Finland, Germany, France, Italy, Spain and the United Kingdom (316 million in 1993) or the combined population of Mexico, Brazil, Argentina and Colombia (313 million in 1993) or more than 11 per cent higher than the combined population of the United States and Canada (287 million in 1993). The second major feature of income-poverty as measured by NSS data on

---

[1] As poverty lines are calculated separately for each state, this figure is the implicit all-India poverty line (Malhotra, 1997).

[2] Estimate based on the Expert Group methodology (Gupta 1999).

TABLE 3.1 *All India estimates of the number and proportion of population below the official poverty line, 1983 to 1997 (per cent)*

Year	Rural	Urban	Combined	Number of persons (in millions)
1983	45.6	40.8	44.5	322.8
1987–88	39.1	38.2	38.9	304.9
1989–90	33.7	36.0	34.3	276
1990–91	35.0	35.3	35.1	291
1992	41.7	37.8	40.7	348
1993–94	37.3	32.4	35.1	320.5
1994–95	38.0	34.2	36.9	329.5
1995–96	38.3	30.0	36.1	328
1997	38.5	33.9	37.2	348.8

Source Gupta (1999), Table 1.

expenditure is that the population of the income-poor in India actually increased by 15.6 million people between 1987–88 and 1993–94, from 304.9 million to 320.5 million (Table 3.1).

The head-count ratio or the proportion of the population that is below the official poverty line declined in most states and at the all-India level during the 1980s. This trend, however, was reversed in the early 1990s, and the most recent estimates point to stagnation in the incidence of poverty (Table 3.1). The absolute numbers of poor persons, however, has risen further – by 28 million between 1993–94 and 1997. These numbers show that public policy has made very little impact on the mass scale of income poverty in India.

Cereal consumption

Cereals are the main source of calories, particularly for consumers in rural areas. Estimates of cereal consumption are available from the NSS and the NNMB.

National Sample Survey data
The NSS conducts regular quinquennial (five-yearly) surveys of household consumer expenditure and these provide information on the quantity of consumption. Information on consumption is collected for a 30-day reference period in four rounds over the year. In the NSS, food items are grouped into ten categories: cereals, roots and tubers; sugars and honey;

TABLE 3.2 *Monthly per capita consumption of cereals, rural and urban areas (kilograms)*

State	Rural			Urban		
	1961–62	*1990–91*	*1993–94*	*1961–62*	*1990–91*	*1993–94*
Andhra Pradesh	16.6	13.62	13.27	13.30	11.70	11.3
Assam	17.06	13.68	13.17	12.39	12.08	12.05
Bihar	18.08	16.45	14.31	15.13	12.85	12.82
Gujarat	15.75	11.75	n.a.	10.63	9.55	n.a.
Haryana	18.3	14.15	12.92	12.21	10.11	10.46
Jammu & Kashmir	22.48	n.a.	n.a.	16.63	n.a.	n.a.
Karnataka	19.79	11.62	13.15	13.22	10.40	10.87
Kerala	9.92	10.73	10.11	10.05	9.60	10.01
Madhya Pradesh	20.9	15.22	14.2	12.99	11.54	11.32
Maharashtra	16.07	11.48	11.39	10.81	9.79	9.37
Orissa	18.22	15.98	15.93	15.00	13.93	13.36
Punjab	18.3	11.69	10.78	12.22	9.06	8.92
Rajasthan	22.25	15.75	14.85	15.23	12.03	11.52
Tamil Nadu	15.71	12.2	11.72	12.77	10.14	10.05
Uttar Pradesh	18.3	14.79	13.91	12.90	11.14	11.08
West Bengal	15.97	15.06	14.96	12.26	11.78	11.64
All India	17.55	14.21	13.4	12.50	10.90	10.63

Source Suryanarayana (1996, 1997).

pulses, nuts and oilseeds; vegetables and fruits; meat, eggs and fish; milk and milk products; oils and fats; miscellaneous foods and beverages; and alcoholic beverages. The data on food intake can also be converted into nutrients (proteins, fats, carbohydrates, vitamins and minerals).

Households are grouped by the NSS into classes or categories according to the level of per capita consumer expenditure. The expenditure categories are defined so as to group households approximately into deciles (that is, the bottom 10 per cent, the next 10 per cent of households and so on). At the very top and bottom of the expenditure scale, however, the categories are smaller and refer to quintiles (or 5 per cent of households).

Table 3.2 indicates that average cereal consumption per capita is low and has declined from 17.5 kg. a month in 1952 to 13.4 kg. in 1993–94 in rural areas. Table 3.2 shows the monthly per capita consumption of cereals in different states for selected years in rural and urban areas respectively. Between 1961–62 and 1990–91, with the exception of rural Kerala, per capita consumption of cereals declined, on average, in every state in both rural and urban areas. From 1990–91 to 1993–94, cereal consumption fell in all states except Karnataka and the urban areas of Kerala.

Data on consumption by expenditure decile shows that the consumption of cereals fell in all decile groups in urban areas and all other than the first decile in rural areas between 1960–61 and 1993–94 (Suryanarayana 1995, 1997). In the lowest decile of rural areas, there was a small fall in consumption between 1987–88 and 1993–94.[3]

Further, over the last two decades, there has been a clear change in the pattern of consumption, with a shift from food to non-food items, and within food, from cereals to other food products. Cereal consumption has declined across all income groups despite a small rise in incomes and a fall in real prices.[4] This shift in consumer behaviour is usually explained as arising from a change in tastes or preferences and in response to changes in relative prices. However, the changes may be 'forced' in that they occur in response to larger changes in the economy (Suryanarayana, 1995). A rise in the share of cash wages and the associated rise in market dependence for acquisition of food, for example, can affect the pattern of consumption (in particular, can lead to a reduction in the consumption of coarse grains). From the nutritional point of view, the observed shift from cereals to other food items among persons with low calorie intakes is likely to exacerbate undernourishment.

National Nutrition Monitoring Bureau data

Nutritional surveys undertaken at regular intervals by the National Nutrition Monitoring Bureau (NNMB) confirm the inadequacy of food (and cereal) intake by large parts of the population. There are two recent surveys conducted by the NNMB that provide data for 1990–91 and 1993–94.[5] The data from these two surveys on the average intake of cereals and millet per consumption unit per day are reported in Table 3.3. In four of

---

[3] In a more detailed examination of these data, by decile and by state, Suryaranarayana (1997) has shown that the decline in consumption was larger for persons in the higher expenditure deciles. Nevertheless, it is a matter of concern that consumption has fallen among groups with very low levels of expenditure, among whom initial consumption levels would have been low.

[4] The decline in total cereal consumption is mainly on account of a decline in the consumption of coarse cereals.

[5] In 1990–91, NNMB undertook a survey in 10 states using the NSSO sampling frame. In 1993–94, a survey was conducted in 8 states using a sampling frame from the NCAER survey on Human Development.

TABLE 3.3 *Average intake of cereals and millets (grams/consumption unit/day)*

State	1991-92	1993-94
Orissa	598.3	524
West Bengal	528.1	n.a.
Karnataka	529.8	496
Andhra Pradesh	523.3	542
Madhya Pradesh	n.a.	539
Tamil Nadu	448.3	394
Gujarat	407.1	445
Maharashtra	390.3	416
Kerala	371.7	366
Pooled	476	464
Balanced daily requirement	460	460

Source NNMB (1993, 1996).

the eight states in which the survey was conducted in both years, average intake of cereals and millets was below the recommended daily intake of 460 grams. Further, intake declined in four states between 1991–92 and 1993–94 while it rose in three states over the same period.

Calorie intake

Next, we turn to intake in terms of energy units (that is calories or Kcal).

National Sample Survey data

The National Sample Survey Organization has recently released data on the calorie intake per person per day in India's 17 most populous States.[6] The most salient feature of the new data is the deeply disturbing finding that, *at the all India level, average calorie intake declined steadily in rural and urban areas between 1972–73 and 1993–94.* The data on average calorie intakes (Figures 3.1 and 3.2 on pp. 20–21) and changes in intakes across states (Figures 3.3 and 3.4 on pp. 22–23) are illustrated in graphs.

In rural India, average calorie intake fell from 2,266 Kcal in 1972–73

---

[6] The discussion in this section is drawn from Swaminathan and Ramachandran (1999). The article was based on data from a paper titled "A Note on Nutritional Intake in India: NSS-50th Round (July 1993 to June 1994)", published in *Sarvekshana*, (NSSO, 1997b). The paper provides data from the 50th Round of the NSS as well as comparative material from the 27th round, conducted in 1972–73, and the 38th round, conducted in 1983.

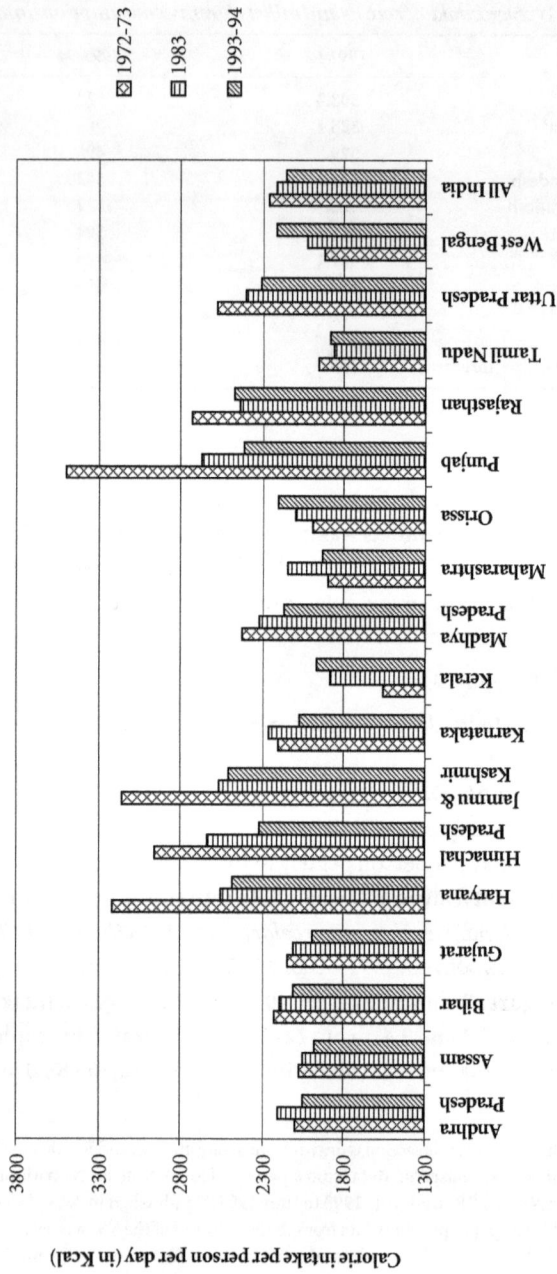

FIGURE 3.1 *Calorie intake per person per day, rural areas, 17 States and India, 1972–73 to 1993–94*

Calorie intake per person per day (in Kcal)

3800 3300 2800 2300 1800 1300

Andhra Pradesh
Assam
Bihar
Gujarat
Haryana
Himachal Pradesh
Jammu & Kashmir
Karnataka
Kerala
Madhya Pradesh
Maharashtra
Orissa
Punjab
Rajasthan
Tamil Nadu
Uttar Pradesh
West Bengal
All India

1972-73
1983
1993-94

Source National Sample Survey, 27th, 38th and 50th Rounds.

FIGURE 3.2 *Calorie intake per person per day, urban areas, 17 States and India, 1972–73 to 1993–94*

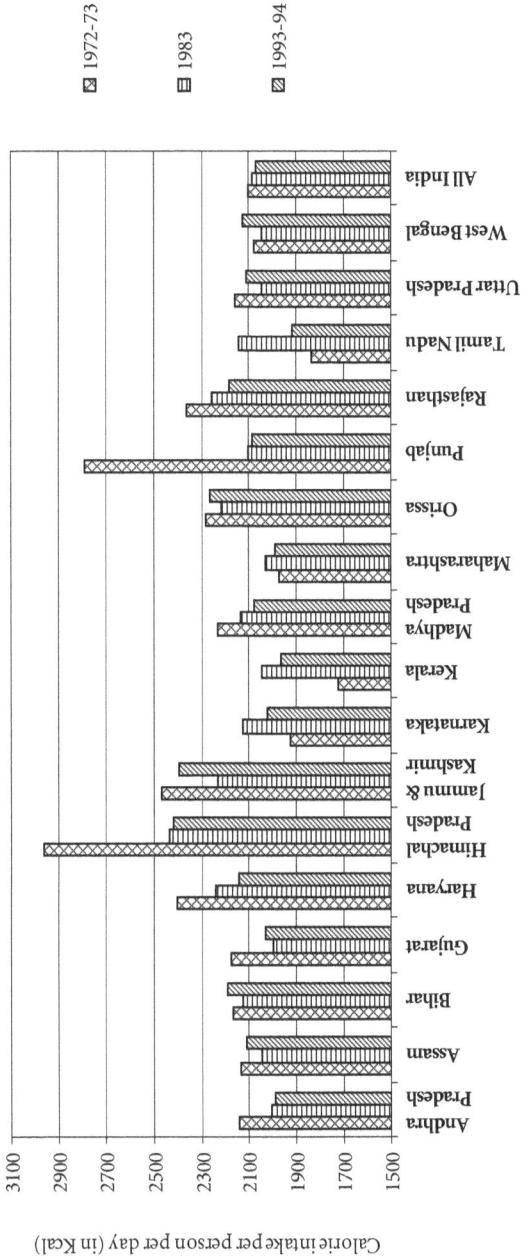

Legend:
- 1972–73
- 1983
- 1993–94

Y-axis: Calorie intake per person per day (in Kcal)

Y-axis values: 1500, 1700, 1900, 2100, 2300, 2500, 2700, 2900, 3100

X-axis categories: Andhra Pradesh, Assam, Bihar, Gujarat, Haryana, Himachal Pradesh, Jammu & Kashmir, Karnataka, Kerala, Madhya Pradesh, Maharashtra, Orissa, Punjab, Rajasthan, Tamil Nadu, Uttar Pradesh, West Bengal, All India

Source National Sample Survey, 27th, 38th and 50th Rounds.

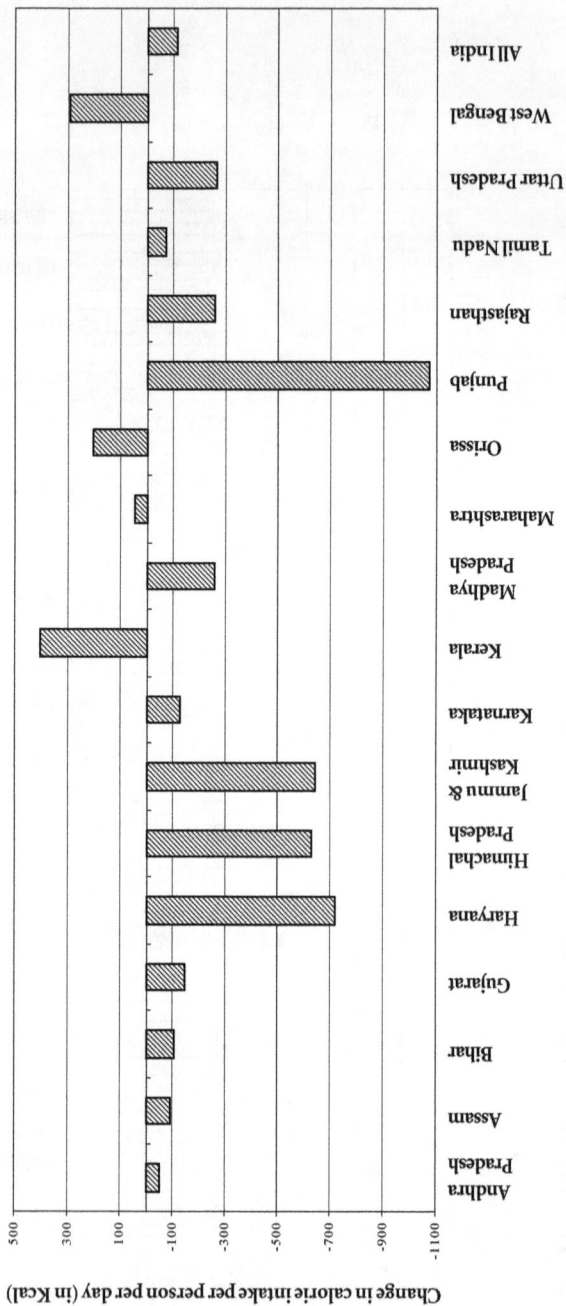

FIGURE 3.3 *Change in calorie intake per person per day between 1972–73 and 1993–94, rural areas, 17 States and India*

Source National Sample Survey, 27th, 38th and 50th Rounds.

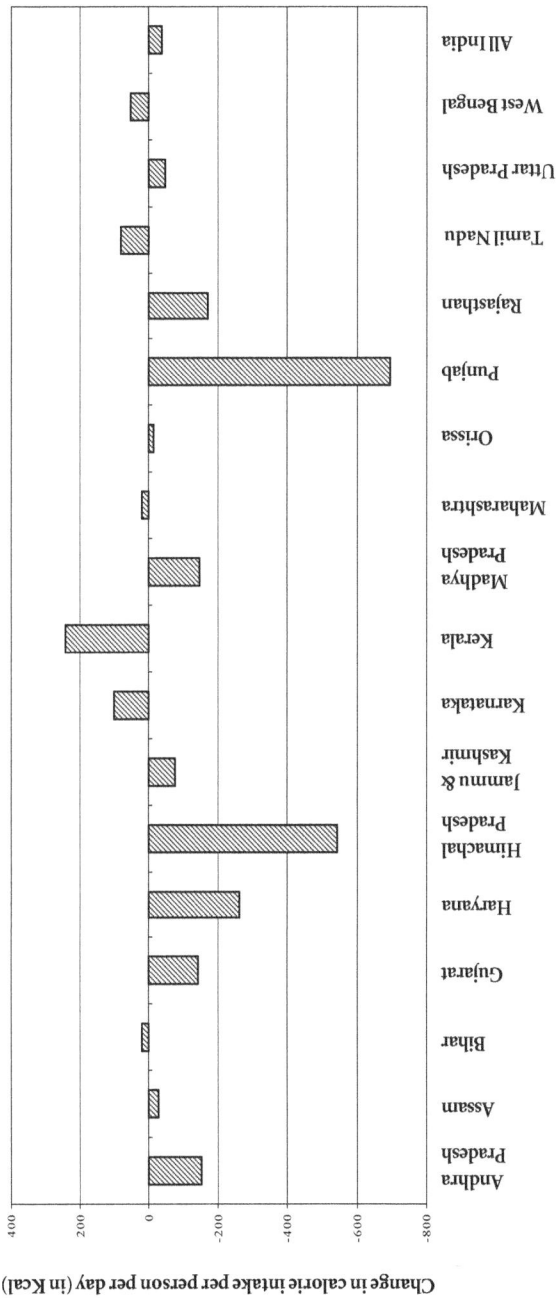

FIGURE 3.4 *Change in calorie intake per person per day between 1972–73 and 1993–94, urban areas, 17 States and India*

Source National Sample Survey, 27th, 38th and 50th Rounds.

TABLE 3.4 *Energy surplus and deficit by expenditure class, all India, rural and urban areas, 1993–94 (Kcal)*

Rural Expenditure class (MPCE in Rs)	Rural Energy Deficit (Kcal) (Norm: 2400 Kcal)	Urban Expenditure Class (MPCE in Rs)	Urban Energy Deficit (Kcal) (Norm: 2100 Kcal)
Less than 120	–1099	Less than 160	–838
120–140	–856	160–190	–618
140–165	–689	190–230	–498
165–190	–590	230–265	–411
190–210	–480	265–310	–325
210–235	–402	310–355	–225
235–265	–293	355–410	–159
265–300	–181	410–490	–68
300–355	–43	490–605	19
355–455	135	605–825	163
455–560	339	825–1055	292
Above 560	775	Above 1055	562
All classes	–300	All classes	–176

Source Shariff and Mallik (1999) Table 6, page 1793.
Note MPCE stands for monthly per capita total expenditure.

to 2,221 in 1983 and to 2,153 in 1993–94. In urban India, the average intake was lower than in rural India. At the same time, the reduction in intake was smaller in urban India than in rural India: intake in urban India went down from 2,107 Kcal in 1972–73 to 2,089 in 1983 and 2,071 in 1993–94.

The fact of declining calorie intakes is of significance and concern because intake by large sections of the population remains below the norm or desired level of consumption. Using NSS data, Shariff and Mallik (1999) calculate the energy deficit for households in different expenditure groups (Table 3.4). Their findings are striking: in 1993–94, on average, persons in 80 per cent of rural households and 70 per cent of urban households were getting less than the recommended amount of calories per day (that is, less than 2,400 calories in rural areas and 2,100 calories in urban areas). In short, except for the top 20–30 per cent of households, there was an energy deficit in the consumption of all other classes. Further, the deficiency (or extent of shortfall from the norm) *increased* in rural areas between 1987–88 and 1993–94 (ibid.).

TABLE 3.*5 Proportion of households with calorie inadequacy, by State (per cent)*

State	1991–92	1993–94
Kerala	47.8	38.7
Tamil Nadu	54.3	70.3
Karnataka	35.7	48.2
Andhra Pradesh	37.5	31.4
Maharastra	60.0	52.1
Gujarat	55.3	39.7
Madhya Pradesh	n.a.	40.1
Orissa	31.2	50.8
West Bengal	31.5	n.a.
Pooled	44.2	47.7

Source NNMB (1993, 1996).

National Nutrition Monitoring Bureau data

Data from the NNMB show that on average 44 per cent of households were characterized by inadequate calorie intake in 1991–92, and the proportion had risen to 47.7 per cent in 1993–94 (Table 3.5). In Tamil Nadu, there was a very sharp rise in calorie inadequacy; 54 per cent of households were calorie deficient in 1991–92 and the corresponding proportion was as high as 70 per cent in 1993–94. In 1991–92, average calorie intake was below the recommended level of 2,350 Kcal a day in 7 states (Maharashtra, Gujarat, Kerala, Karnataka, Andhra Pradesh, Tamil Nadu and West Bengal) out of the 8 states surveyed (see Table 3.6 overleaf). Orissa was the exception but by 1993–94, average intake was below the norm in Orissa as well. The only state with an average intake above the recommended daily norm in 1993–94 was Andhra Pradesh.

Micronutrient intake

Another dimension of hunger, also referred to as 'hidden hunger', is the inadequate intake of micronutrients, which play a critical role in body functioning. The NNMB survey of 1991–92 showed that 'diets were deficit in all the micronutrients (iron, vitamin A, thiamine, riboflavin, niacin and vitamin C) except calcium in 6 out of 8 states surveyed' (NNMB 1993: 21). In the case of vitamin A, for example, mean intakes ranged from 197 μg in Kerala to 368 μg in West Bengal. The recommended daily intake of vitamin A is 600 μg. The incidence of nutrient deficiencies did not change between 1991–92 and 1993–94. The nutrient deficit was highest for vitamin

TABLE 3.6 *Average energy intake (Kcal)*

State	1991-92	1993-94
Maharashtra	1922	2065
West Bengal	2297	n.a
Karnataka	2293	2196
Andhra Pradesh	2247	2430
Kerala	2055	2231
Gujarat	1969	2298
Tamil Nadu	1950	1814
Orissa	2397	2106
Madhya Pradesh	n.a	2238
Recommended daily intake	2350	2350

Source NNMB (1993, 1996).

A, followed by riboflavin. In most states, 90 per cent of households had an inadequate intake of vitamin A.

Nutritional outcomes

In addition to measuring the quantity of food consumption and calorie intake, we can examine the nutritional status of individuals and identify whether they are adequately nourished. NNMB reports provide inform-ation on nutritional outcomes, both among children and among adults, in different parts of the country.

Adult nutrition

A commonly used indicator of undernutrition among adults is the Body Mass Index (BMI), defined as the ratio of weight (in kilograms) to the square of height (in metres).[7] A value for the BMI of 18.5 or more is taken to indicate normal nutritional status. The cut-off is the same for men and women. If the BMI is taken as an indicator of undernutrition, then, as shown in Table 3.7, 46 per cent of men and women were chronically energy deficient in 1991–92 (that is, their BMI fell below 18.5) in the surveyed states. Severe undernutrition (a BMI less than 16) was observed among 9 per cent of adult men and 10 per cent of adult women. The pooled data for 1993–94 indicate that 48 per cent of adults, men and women together, were undernourished. In other words, in terms of the BMI criterion, *about*

---

[7] The BMI is held to be a good choice for the anthropometric assessment of the nutritional status of adults (Shetty and James, 1994). Shetty and James (1994) also provide the different cut-off points.

TABLE 3.7 *Proportion of adults with chronic energy deficiency, by sex and State (BMI criterion)*

State	1991–92		1993–94
	Male	*Female*	*Both*
Kerala	36.97	27.78	33.2
Tamil Nadu	42.06	45.05	37.3
Karnataka	52.11	53.19	53.8
Andhra Pradesh	41.31	47.35	49.4
Maharastra	52.86	54.89	51.0
Gujarat	56.82	49.04	53.1
Madhya Pradesh	n.a.	n.a.	53.3
Orissa	43.8	49.15	57.3
West Bengal	42.65	44.47	n.a.
Pooled States	46.02	45.84	48.5

Source NNMB (1993, 1996).
Note A BMI of less than 18.5 denotes chronic energy deficiency.

one-half of the adult population in the country is malnourished. Moreover, between 1991–92 and 1993–94, there was a rise in the incidence of adult malnutrition in Orissa, Andhra Pradesh and Karnataka.

Child nutrition

The nutritional status of children is usually measured on the basis of a weight-for-age criterion. A child of a given age (in months) and sex is said to be moderately undernourished if his/her weight falls below two standard deviations of the median in the reference population. A child is severely malnourished if her weight falls below three standard deviations of the norm. The World Health Organization (WHO) has provided reference norms based on data for a healthy population. An alternative reference norm is that provided by the National Centre for Health Statistics (NCHS) in the United States.

National Nutrition Monitoring Bureau data

For children in the age group from birth to five, the pooled NNMB data (that is, for all states surveyed) show that 55 per cent of girls and 57 per cent of boys were malnourished in 1991–92 (Table 3.8 overleaf).[8] In terms

---

[8] The nutritional status of girls was worse than that of boys in some states (such as Tamil Nadu and Orissa) but boys were worse off than girls in several other states (including Kerala) were.

TABLE 3.8 *Moderate and severe malnutrition among children age 1 to 5 years, by State and sex, 1991–92 and 1993–94 (weight-for-age criterion)*

State		1991–92			1993–94
		Moderate	Severe	Severe + Moderate	Severe + Moderate
Kerala	Boys	29.5	6.3	35.8	34.4
	Girls	29.9	5.7	35.6	34.2
	All children	29.6	6	35.6	
Tamil Nadu	Boys	42.1	6.4	48.5	40.5
	Girls	50.6	5	55.6	39.7
	All children	46.7	5.7	52.4	
Karnataka	Boys	57	7.7	64.7	55.6
	Girls	51.7	8.9	60.6	51.1
	All children	54.5	8.3	62.8	
Andhra Pradesh	Boys	44.9	10.6	55.5	48.6
	Girls	38.8	7.1	45.9	49.6
	All children	41.9	8.9	50.8	
Maharastra	Boys	43	23	66	52.7
	Girls	46.9	10.9	57.8	55.6
	All children	44.9	17.3	62.2	
Gujarat	Boys	54.8	9.6	64.4	74.2
	Girls	45.7	14.7	60.4	61.8
	All children	50.8	11.9	62.7	
Madhya Pradesh	Boys	n.a.	n.a.	n.a.	57.9
	Girls	n.a.	n.a.	n.a.	49.6
	All children				
Orissa	Boys	41.8	11	52.8	55.1
	Girls	43.2	15.5	58.7	51.4
	All children	42.5	13.3	55.8	
West Bengal	Boys	41.3	19.3	60.6	n.a.
	Girls	43.8	16.8	60.6	n.a.
	All children	42.7	17.9	60.6	
All States	Boys	45.6	11.6	57.2	n.a.
	Girls	44.6	10.5	55.1	n.a.
	All children	45.1	11.1	56.2	

Source NNMB (1993, 1996).

Note Moderate malnutrition is defined as weight-for-age falling between 60 and 75 per cent of the NCHS norm, and severe malnutrition is defined as weight-for-age less than 60 per cent of the norm.

of changes over time, for the seven states that were surveyed in both years, the patterns are mixed. There was an unambiguous decline in the incidence of undernutrition in a few states – Kerala, Tamil Nadu, Karnataka and Maharashtra. The incidence of child undernutrition increased in states such as Orissa and Gujarat. It is perturbing, however, that the overall trend was *not* one of a steady decline in the prevalence of undernutrition among young children.

National Family Health Survey data

An alternative source of information on the nutritional status of children is the National Family Health Survey (NFHS), which was conducted in 24 states in 1992–93 (IIPS, 1995). The NFHS estimated the nutritional status of children in the age group 0–4 on the basis of anthropometric measurements of height and weight. When a weight-for-age criterion was used, 53 per cent of boys and girls were found to be undernourished and 21 per cent of the children surveyed were found to be severely undernourished.[9] Table 3.9 (overleaf) summarizes the information for 25 surveyed states. The extent of severe malnutrition was lowest in Kerala (boys: 5.4 %; girls: 6.9%) and the highest in Bihar (boys: 33%; girls: 29%). In terms of overall malnutrition (moderate or severe), Kerala, Mizoram and Nagaland were the only states where less than 30 per cent of children were undernourished. The incidence of malnutrition was extremely high in Bihar (62.6%).

Food Shares

The importance of food shares is illustrated by the importance given to this measure by public policy in different countries. In the United States, the Food Stamp programme is a major food subsidy programme, with around 27 million monthly participants in 1995 and total expenditures of more than $24 billion a year. To be eligible for food stamps, households are identified with respect to a specific poverty line. The original standard for the poverty line, developed in 1964, was based on requirements for food expenditure and the poverty line was roughly thrice the estimated food expenditure (with adjustments for household size and composition) as it was shown that poor families spend about one-third of their expenditure on food.[10] In short, any household that spends more than one-third

---

[9] The norm is based on the median of the reference population as stipulated by the WHO.

[10] The lowest income quintile spends about 33 per cent of income on food as compared to under 10 per cent by the highest income quintile (Kuhn et al., 1996).

TABLE 3.9 *Proportion of undernourished children, ages 1-47 months, 1992-93 (weight-for-age criterion)*

State	Boys		Girls		All children	
	Severe	Moderate	Severe	Moderate	Severe	Moderate
Andhra Pradesh	13.8	47.1	17.5	51.1	15.6	49.1
Assam	19.4	52.4	18.0	48.5	18.7	50.4
Bihar	33.1	64.9	29.1	60.4	31.1	62.6
Delhi	12.7	41.6	11.3	41.6	12	41.6
Gujarat	15.0	41.6	14.9	46.7	17.6	50.1
Haryana	7.5	34.9	10.8	41.6	9	37.9
Himachal Pradesh	11.2	47.8	14.8	46.1	12.9	47
Jammu and Kashmir	11.8	41.6	15.9	47.5	13.8	44.5
Karnataka	18.4	52.9	20.5	55.0	19.4	54.3
Kerala	5.4	28.8	6.9	28.3	6.1	28.5
Madhya Pradesh	17.6	53.0	20.4	49.1	22.3	57.4
Maharashtra	18.5	51.3	22.0	54.0	21.3	54.2
Orissa	22.0	53.4	23.6	53.2	22.7	53.3
Punjab	13.6	43.9	14.8	47.9	14.2	45.9
Rajasthan	18.4	42.5	20.2	40.5	19.2	41.6
Tamil Nadu	11.5	43.1	13.8	49.7	13.3	48.2
Uttar Pradesh	19.3	51.8	19.2	47.8	24.6	59
West Bengal	17.2	54.7	19.6	59.0	18.4	56.8
Arunachal Pradesh					14.5	39.7
Manipur					7.2	30.1
Meghalaya					17.2	45.5
Mizoram					5.3	28.1
Nagaland					7.6	28.7
Tripura					18.6	48.8
Goa					8.9	35.0
All India	20.2	53.3	21.0	53.4	20.6	53.4

Source National Family Health Survey 1992-93.
Note Moderate malnutrition occurs when weight-for-age is less than two standard deviations of the WHO norm, and severe malnutrition occurs when weight-for-age is less than three standard deviations of the norm.

of its income on food is considered 'poor' for purposes of the Food Stamp programme (Kuhn et al., 1996).

National Sample survey estimates of food shares for households in different expenditure deciles in 1993–94 are shown in Table 3.10. First, in rural areas, for the bottom half of the population, food shares were over 70 per cent. For the next four deciles, food shares were between 60 and 70 per cent. It is only for those in the top five per cent that the food share was below 50 per cent. By any standard, food is the most important item of

TABLE 3.10 *Food shares (or food expenditure as a proportion of total expenditure) by expenditure decile, all India, rural and urban areas, 1993–94 (per cent)*

Expenditure decile	Rural	Urban
0–10	73.1	70.6
10–20	73.1	69.6
20–30	72.3	67.6
30–40	71.6	65.8
40–50	70.3	63.9
50–60	69.3	62.1
60–70	67.4	59.4
70–80	65.5	55.8
80–90	61.9	52.3
90–95	57.0	48.3
95–100	42.4	34.5
Computed average	67.4	60.8
Simple Mean/All	63.1	54.6

Source Computed from National Sample Survey Organisation (1997a), *Consumption of Some Important Commodities in India, NSS 50th round, 1993–94.*

Note Deciles are based on households ranked by total consumer expenditure.

expenditure for the overwhelming majority of rural households.[11] In urban areas, food shares were lower in every decile than food shares in rural areas. Food shares were higher than 60 per cent for those in the bottom six deciles and above 50 per cent for those in the next three deciles. For the richest 5 per cent of the population, food expenditure was about one-third of total expenditure. So if we used the criterion of the Food Stamp programme in India, around 95 per cent of all households would be 'poor'. Alternatively, if we used a food share of 60 per cent to identify the poor, the cut-off that is used in China to identify a poverty line,[12] then 80 per cent of the rural population and 60 per cent of the urban population would be 'poor'.

Summing up

The evidence presented above demonstrates that food deprivation and poverty persist on a mass scale in India today. First, in 1993–94, about 320 million people (or 35 per cent of the population) had consumption

---

[11] Although the food share has been declining slowly for households in all expenditure deciles including the lowest deciles, the size of the food share remains very high.

[12] Wang Youjuan (1999), 'Some Issues of Urban Poverty in China' cited in Li Shi (1999).

expenditures below the official poverty line. Secondly, the consumption of cereals, the major source of energy, has, on average, declined. Thirdly, calorie intakes are low, and a large proportion of individuals fail to obtain the minimum daily requirement of calories. According to NSS data for 1993–94, the intake of calories was deficient for 70–80 per cent of households in India. Fourthly, a large number of persons suffer deficiencies in the consumption of micronutrients. Fifthly, in terms of nutritional status based on anthropometric measures, about 50 per cent of adults and 55 per cent of children are undernourished. Lastly, expenditure on food accounts for the bulk of total expenditure in a very large majority of households: food expenditure is more than 60 per cent of household expenditure for 80 per cent of rural households and 60 per cent of urban households.

These findings have significant implications for the debate on the PDS, both in terms of the need for the PDS and, more importantly, in terms of the number and proportion of the population that should have access to the PDS. The first significant conclusion is that *the proportion of persons suffering deprivations in food and nutrition is higher than the proportion defined as being income-poor or below the official poverty line.* While around 37 per cent of rural households were below the poverty line in 1993–94, 80 per cent of households showed a calorie deficit. Secondly, if the objective of a system such as the PDS is to reduce food insecurity, then it should be available both to those currently undernourished as well as to those who face a risk of undernourishment. While anthropometric measures suggest that 50 per cent of adults are undernourished, the data on food consumption and calorie intake show that over 70 per cent of households are deficient in food consumption.

Evidence on the consumption of food, on calorie intake, and on nutritional outcomes clearly establishes that chronic hunger persists on a mass scale in India. The persistence of hunger and malnutrition, and of vulnerability to hunger and malnutrition, on such a scale is the principal justification for strengthening a system of food distribution such as PDS.

four

What Ails PDS Today?

Failures and Successes of PDS in India

There is little doubt that PDS as it functions today has failed to provide cheap food and food security on a mass scale to households that are undernourished or vulnerable to undernourishment. In this chapter, we examine certain features of PDS, specifically the coverage or reach of PDS and its variations across states and over time. In doing so, the chapter brings out the enormous disparities in the functioning of PDS in different parts of the country. The failures of PDS, as outlined here, however, do not constitute an argument against a system of food distribution controlled by the public authority. Far from it: our objective is to find ways of restructuring PDS to make it an effective tool of food and nutrition security. We need to learn lessons from the failures of PDS and from its successes. The experience of Kerala, discussed on page 58, provides an example of an effective system of public delivery of food. It also shows that the creation and continuation of an effective system of food security requires political commitment and public support – government support and support from below.

The chapter is structured as follows. The section below examines the coverage of PDS in different states on the basis of information on aggregate quantities of food grain distributed through PDS. There is a small digression on the degree of urban bias in the delivery of food through PDS. The following section examines the utilization of PDS by different economic classes or categories of households in different states. For this analysis, I draw upon available national survey data as well as data reported by village studies. In the next section, problems of administration are outlined in brief, and the section after that examines the impact of PDS on food prices. This is followed by a discussion of the Kerala experience.

Coverage of PDS across states

To understand the variations in the utilization of PDS, we examine the quantities of food grain (namely rice and wheat) allocated and distributed in different states and over time. The analysis brings out the non-uniformity in coverage of PDS across regions and over time. Let me clarify a few terms. 'Quantity allocated' refers to the amount of rice or wheat allotted from the central pool to a certain state. 'Quantity of offtake' refers to the amount that is actually purchased by the state and then distributed to fair-price shops. At the central level, in addition to allocating food grain to PDS, food grain is also allocated for defence services, for employment schemes, noon meal programmemes, and so on. Such allocations are not included in our discussion. With a few exceptions all the quantities refer to quantities supplied (allocation or offtake) and not to the quantity actually demanded or purchased by consumers. If there are no leakages, the quantity supplied will be equivalent to the quantity purchased by consumers.

Regional variations in total offtake and per capita offtake

There are large regional differences in the scale and operation of PDS, and these can clearly be observed from data on the total offtake of food grain in PDS in different states in 1995 (Table 4.1). The four southern states, Andhra Pradesh, Tamil Nadu, Kerala, and Karnataka, stand out in terms of the distribution of food grain, accounting for almost one-half (48.7 per cent) of total PDS offtake of food grain in the country. In terms of total quantities, the highest quantity of cereal distributed was in Andhra Pradesh, followed by Tamil Nadu. After Andhra Pradesh, Tamil Nadu and Kerala, the largest share of offtake was in West Bengal. By comparison, the four northern states of Bihar, Madhya Pradesh, Rajasthan, and Uttar Pradesh (or BIMARU states) accounted together for only 10 per cent of total offtake.

TABLE 4.1 *Total sales or offtake of food grain in the PDS and population, all States and Union Territories, 1995*

State/U.T.	Share of State in all India population (per cent)	Population (in 000s)	Quantity of offtake (in 000 tonnes)			Share of State in all India offtake of food grain (per cent)
			Rice	Wheat	Food grain	
Andhra Pradesh	7.8	71712	2322	110	2432	17.1
Tamil Nadu	6.4	58287	1560	160	1720	12.1
Kerala	3.4	30907	1149	499	1648	11.6
West Bengal	8.0	73271	455	845	1300	9.2
Karnataka	5.2	48054	896	232	1128	7.9
Maharashtra	9.4	85905	317	602	919	6.5
Assam	2.7	24610	408	357	765	5.4
Gujarat	4.9	44614	202	427	629	4.4
Orissa	3.7	34268	326	200	526	3.7
Rajasthan	5.3	48205	9	484	493	3.5
Uttar Pradesh	16.4	150118	208	226	434	3.1
Jammu & Kashmir	0.9	8505	262	113	375	2.6
Madhya Pradesh	7.9	72139	194	140	334	2.3
Bihar	10.4	94907	19	198	217	1.5
Meghalaya	0.2	1960	156	28	184	1.3
Delhi	1.2	10965	30	160	190	1.3
Tripura	0.3	3045	161	8	169	1.2
Himachal Pradesh	0.6	5611	44	109	153	1.1
Mizoram	0.1	789	96	25	121	0.8
Arunachal Pradesh	0.1	961	90	9	99	0.7
Nagaland	0.15	1386	68	36	104	0.7
Goa	0.1	1273	42	22	64	0.5
Haryana	1.9	18072	7	53	60	0.4
Manipur	0.2	2031	29	28	57	0.4
Sikkim	0.05	467	42	10	52	0.4
Lakshadweep		58	4	Neg	4	0.03
Punjab	2.4	21599	1	2	3	0.02
Pondicherry	0.1	882	3	Neg	3	0.02
Chandigarh		777	1	–	1	0.01
D & N Haveli		156	1	–	1	0.01
Daman & Diu		111	1	–	1	0.01
A & N Islands	0.2*	328	–	–	–	–
All India		915971	9103	5083	14186	100

Note Data refer to actual sales from central pool to various state governments, as reported by the Ministry of Food, and do not include sales to the Defence Ministry, BSF etc. Food grain, here, refers to rice and wheat together.

* Is the combined population share of Andaman and Nicobar islands, Chandigarh, Dadra and Nagar Haveli, Daman and Diu and Lakshadweep.

Source *Bulletin on Food Statistics 1994–95.*

TABLE 4.2 *Total sales or offtake of food grain in the PDS, all States and Union Territories, 1998 (thousand tonnes)*

State/U.T.	Rice	Wheat	Total food grain	Share of state in all India offtake of food grain
Andhra Pradesh	1991.4	132	2123.4	11.5
Tamil Nadu	1273	246.3	1519.3	8.2
Kerala	1653.6	472.6	2126.2	11.5
West Bengal	248.2	1020.2	1268.4	6.8
Karnataka	890.6	306.7	1197.3	6.5
Maharashtra	630.5	1082.5	1713	9.3
Assam	548.6	232.7	781.3	4.2
Gujarat	227.6	425.1	652.7	3.5
Orissa	585	406	991	5.4
Rajasthan	4.9	481.5	486.4	2.6
Uttar Pradesh	426.9	1003.8	1430.7	7.7
Jammu & Kashmir	277.9	147.6	425.5	2.3
Madhya Pradesh	299.4	324.2	623.8	3.4
Bihar	233.5	689.9	923.4	5.0
Meghalaya	179.6	28.8	208.4	1.1
Delhi	111.9	611.6	723.5	3.9
Tripura	174.2	17.7	191.9	1.0
Himachal Pradesh	108.7	130.3	239	1.3
Mizoram	119	23.6	142.6	0.8
Arunachal Pradesh	92.4	5.6	98	0.5
Nagaland	114.2	42.1	156.3	0.8
Goa	62.2	33.5	95.7	0.5
Haryana	0	102.8	102.8	0.6
Manipur	46.2	30.8	77	0.4
Sikkim	58.4	9.4	67.8	0.4
Lakshadweep	3.9	0.3	4.2	0.0
Punjab	1.6	9	10.6	0.1
Pondicherry	1	0.1	1.1	0.0
Chandigarh	2.1	5.1	7.2	0.0
D & N Haveli	4.4	2.5	6.9	0.0
Daman & Diu	1.6	0.7	2.3	0.0
A & N Islands	0	0	0	0.0
All India	10373	8145	18518@	100.0

Note Data refer to actual sales from central pool to various state governments, as reported by the Ministry of Food, and do not include sales to the Defence Ministry, BSF etc.

@ Due to rounding off errors, this total is not equal to the sum of the column.

The share of each state in the total population of the country is also reported in Table 4.1. It can be seen that the share of food grain offtake is much

TABLE 4.3 *Per capita food grain offtake, per capita SDP and proportion of population below poverty line in selected States,1995*

State/U.T.	Per capita food grain (in kg.), 1995	Per capita SDP at current prices, 1995-96	Proportion of poor, 1993-94
Andhra Pradesh	33.91	8938	22.19
Assam	31.08	6288	40.86
Bihar	2.29	3524	54.96
Goa	50.27	18984	14.92
Gujarat	14.10	11977	24.21
Haryana	3.32	13518	25.05
Himachal Pradesh	27.27	8747	28.44
Jammu & Kashmir	44.09	6181	25.17
Karnataka	23.47	9384	33.16
Kerala	53.32	8324	25.43
Madhya Pradesh	4.63	6518	42.52
Maharashtra	10.70	15457	36.86
Orissa	15.35	6192	48.56
Punjab	0.14	16044	11.77
Rajasthan	10.23	6959	27.41
Tamil Nadu	29.51	9868	35.03
Uttar Pradesh	2.89	5874	40.85
West Bengal	17.74	8409	35.66

Note SDP stands for State Domestic Product. The poverty ratios are taken from GOI (1997).

Source Bulletin on Food Statistics, Economic Survey 1998-99 and GOI (1997).

higher than the share of population for the southern states and a few other states such as Assam, the North-Eastern states, Himachal Pradesh, Jammu and Kashmir and West Bengal. For most other states, including the four BIMARU states, the share of offtake was much lower than their share in total population.

If we examine the data on offtake over the last two decades, we find a relative decline in the share of Maharashtra and West Bengal in total offtake. In 1971, for example, these two states accounted for 43 per cent of PDS offtake (Bhalla, 1994). By 1995, however, the expansion of PDS in the southern states meant that the traditional dominance of Maharashtra and West Bengal, on account of the scale of urban rationing in Mumbai and Calcutta, had disappeared. There have been further changes in the pattern of offtake across states after the introduction of targeting in 1996. Among the top five states, on a ranking by the share of total offtake, the position of all but one declined between 1995 and 1998 (Table 4.2). Kerala was the

TABLE 4.4 *Annual per capita food grain offtake under PDS in selected States,*
1981, 1991 and 1995

State	Annual per capita food grain offtake (kg)					% change	
	1973-89*	1981	1991	1995	1998	1981-1991	1991-98
Andhra Pradesh	13.79	11.00	35.90	33.91	28.58	226.34	-20.39
Assam	28.32	27.00	30.47	31.08	30.40	12.85	-0.23
Bihar	9.46	8.00	6.83	2.29	9.48	-14.67	38.89
Goa			72.22	50.27	63.80		-11.66
Gujarat	16.72	12.00	27.28	14.10	13.80	127.35	-49.42
Haryana	10.71	7.00	10.49	3.32	5.30	49.85	-49.48
Himachal Pradesh	16.88	16.00	36.33	27.27	36.77	127.03	1.22
Jammu & Kashmir	47.72	41.00	47.33	44.09	44.32	15.43	-6.34
Karnataka	19.48	18.00	22.84	23.47	23.38	26.91	2.37
Kerala	51.39	46.00	70.39	53.32	66.65	53.02	-5.31
Madhya Pradesh	8.81	10.00	9.24	4.63	8.02	-7.56	-13.29
Maharashtra	25.81	25.00	24.57	10.70	19.10	-1.73	-22.27
Orissa	12.84	11.00	16.86	15.35	27.99	53.24	66.07
Punjab	13.62	12.00	4.56	0.14	0.46	-61.99	-89.98
Rajasthan	11.56	6.00	20.19	10.23	9.32	236.57	-53.86
Tamil Nadu	24.38	24.00	20.75	29.51	24.91	-13.55	20.04
Uttar Pradesh	7.77	8.00	7.37	2.89	8.68	-7.92	17.78
West Bengal	36.30	38.00	23.41	17.74	16.37	-38.39	-30.09

Note: The north-eastern states have been excluded due to some problems with the
data.
   * Average for 1973–89, taken from Geetha and Suryanarayana (1993) Table 2.
Source: *Bulletin on Food Statistics* and *Economic Survey 1998-99.*

exception and maintained its share of total offtake, but the share of Andhra
Pradesh, Tamil Nadu, West Bengal and Karnataka fell. The decline was
marked for Andhra Pradesh, with its share of total offtake dropping from
17.1 per cent in 1995 to 11.5 per cent in 1998. This decline derives both
from the restructuring of PDS by the government of Andhra Pradesh as
part of its own structural adjustment, and the changes in allocation
stemming from the introduction of the Targeted PDS.

A more accurate picture of differences across states and regions
emerges when we examine the distribution of per capita quantities, that
is, after adjusting for population size. Table 4.3 (p. 37) shows the per capita
cereal offtake in 1995 in different states. In per capita terms, Kerala was
the undoubted leader. In Kerala, the average per capita offtake of grain
from PDS amounted to 53.3 kg. in a year. In sharp contrast, the per capita
offtake was 2.3 kg. in Bihar and 4.6 kg. in Madhya Pradesh. Evidently,

there are huge differences in the scale of operation of PDS in different parts of the country.

These inter-state differences in the scale of PDS operations have persisted over many years. To illustrate, in Table 4.4, we report the per capita offtake of cereals from PDS in 1981, 1991, 1995 and 1998 in the major states as well as the average offtake over the period 1973–89. The figures on average offtake over a long period show that the differences are not on account of any single year deviation. At the same time, when we examine offtake in 1981 and 1991, we find that there were some interesting changes. In 1981, food grain offtake per person was highest in Kerala (46 kg.) and lowest in Rajasthan (6 kg.). In 1991, Kerala was still distributing the highest quantity per capita, over 70 kg. of grain per person per year. In Andhra Pradesh, there was a *huge increase* in offtake, of 226 per cent, between 1981 and 1991, from 11 kg. to 36 kg. per person per year. A big increase also occurred in Rajasthan (though this is probably on account of a lower than average offtake in 1981). In UP and Bihar, there was a *decline* in per capita offtake between 1981 and 1991. Of the 17 states in Table 4.4, per capita offtake declined in 7 states between 1981 and 1991. In other words, during the 1980s, there was an expansion of PDS in certain states, notably the southern states, Gujarat and Himachal Pradesh, and a reduction in certain other states.

The most striking feature of the immediate post-structural adjustment period, from 1991 to 1995, however, is the *widespread decline in per capita offtake.* In as many as 14 states, per capita offtake of food grain fell between 1991 and 1995. The three exceptions were Assam, Karnataka and Tamil Nadu. This trend was reversed between 1995 and 1998, when per capita offtake rose in 10 states. This reversal, as explained in the Chapter 6, is on account of the new Targeted PDS, which resulted in a shift in the quantities allocated to different states. However, if the entire period 1991 to 1998 is considered, the major feature remains the tendency for a fall in per capita offtake. Per capita offtake declined in 12 states, remained unchanged in two states, and rose in only four states (Bihar, Orissa, Tamil Nadu and UP) between 1991 and 1998. Other than Tamil Nadu, the three states in which per capita offtake rose were states with very low offtake historically. The introduction of structural adjustment policies and the impact on PDS offtake in the 1990s is discussed further in Chapter 6.

Poverty, incomes and PDS offtake
We have established that there are big differences in the scale of PDS in different parts of the country. Are these differences on account of differences in the extent of poverty? A quick glance at Table 4.3, in which we have reported the per capita State Domestic Product (or SDP) of different states as well as the incidence of poverty (as reported in official documents), shows that the quantity of per capita offtake is not positively associated with the incidence of poverty. States with higher poverty ratios in 1993–94 were not the states with higher per capita offtake of food grain.[1] Similarly, there is no simple relation between state income and purchases from PDS. These observations are not surprising given that PDS, till recently, was viewed as a programme with universal coverage. The divergences across states in the effectiveness and scale of PDS arise from differences in political commitment to food security, and not from differences in state income or in the incidence of poverty.

Nevertheless, the establishment of PDS has provided some safeguards against worsening of inequalities of consumption across states. Over the last thirty years, although cereal consumption per capita has declined (Chapter 3), inter-state variations in cereal consumption and in calorie intake have declined. The coefficient of variation in per capita monthly cereal consumption in rural areas fell from 13.63 in 1961–62 to 10.39 in 1987–88 (Suryanarayana 1996). PDS is likely to have played a role in the moderation of inequalities in cereal consumption across states.

A digression on urban bias
Many scholars have been concerned about an 'urban bias' in the pattern of allocation of food grain in PDS, and argued that PDS has predominantly served the interests of the urban population and neglected the vast rural population.[2] There are many possible ways of measuring the relative position of rural and urban areas with respect to PDS and some of the controversy has really been about choosing an indicator that provides the best measure of rural–urban bias. The following are some of the indicators that have been used to identify the extent of urban bias in PDS.

---

[1] In fact, the rank correlation coefficient between percentage of population below the poverty line and distribution of food grain through PDS is reported to be negative and insignificant (Bhalla 1994).

[2] See, for example, Dantwala (1976), Dreze and Sen (1990).

• Ratio of rural to urban per capita consumption of food grain from PDS.
• Value of per capita subsidy in rural areas to that in urban areas
• Ratio of rural to urban per capita consumption of PDS grain among markets users. Since many rural households cultivate food crops, their dependence on PDS for food consumption is likely to differ from that of urban households that purchase all the food they consume. In this indicator, only households that make purchases of grain are included.

These indicators were estimated for 18 states with data from the 42nd round of the NSS for 1986–87 (Mahendra Dev and Suryanarayana 1991; Howes and Jha 1992). The first indicator had a value greater than one for seven states (Andhra Pradesh, Gujarat, Himachal Pradesh, Kerala, Rajasthan, Tamil Nadu and Tripura), indicating a rural bias in these states (Howes and Jha 1992). The ratio was below one in the remaining states (indicating that urban per capita consumption was greater than rural per capita consumption), and very low (less than 0.5) in six states. By this measure, there was an urban bias in PDS in a majority of states. The second indicator, which takes account of rural–urban price differentials, also showed an urban bias in 10 out of 18 states (ibid.). The third indicator, however, showed no urban bias at the all-India level although there was a pronounced urban bias in states such as West Bengal and Maharashtra, and a rural bias in states such as Tamil Nadu, Andhra Pradesh and Kerala (Mahendra Dev and Suryanarayana 1991).

The findings vary with the definition of urban bias. Also, the patterns of allocation across rural and urban areas in certain large states influence the all-India pattern of distribution. The important point from this debate is the prevalence of large inter-state variations in the pattern of allocation of food grain. The more pertinent issue, and the one we turn to next, is the extent to which PDS reaches the poor and the undernourished, be they resident in rural locations or urban.

Distribution of PDS across classes

The critical issue, thus, is the pattern of purchase from PDS across economic classes, and the extent to which the income-poor are able to gain access and to benefit from PDS. This issue, however, is difficult to capture, as most official information on PDS is of an aggregate nature and does not provide information on utilization by persons from different economic strata. At the national level, the only available survey of the utilization of PDS by households in different expenditure classes is the one undertaken by the National Sample Survey (NSS) in 1986–87.[3] Although dated, this survey can be a starting point in (a) identifying how many households purchased grain from PDS in different states; and (b) recording the extent of utilization of PDS (or scale of purchase). In both cases, by examining households in different expenditure groups, we can check the extent to which the poor used PDS.[4] The next section deals with the first aspect, termed participation, and the following section deals with the extent of purchase. In both sections, I draw upon data from the NSS survey as well as from village studies.

Participation in PDS

This section identifies to what extent households from different economic strata bought rice and wheat from PDS.

National Sample Survey data
Among those who bought grain from PDS, two categories were demarcated by the NSS: those for whom PDS grain accounted for all the grain they bought and others for whom it accounted for only a part of their purchases of grain. These data were analysed for all states and by household expenditure classes (Parikh 1994). Table 4.5, taken from Parikh (1994), shows the results for the rural population. In UP and Bihar, *around 98 per cent of the rural population did not purchase any grain from PDS,* that is, did not

---

[3] There are problems with the quality of data from this survey, in particular, a mismatch between consumption as reported in this survey and that implied by official data on offtake or supply.

[4] The impact of PDS could also be evaluated in terms of the value of the subsidy transferred to households through the purchase of cheap or low-price grain. The equivalence of a ration with a lump sum income transfer is a standard assumption among economists (Besley and Kanbur, 1988). This assumption may, however, be questioned on many grounds, among them, various arguments in favour of in-kind transfers (in this case, for instance, the direct nutritional value of food), and practical concerns such as the ability to make compensating lump sum income transfers. Given these problems with measuring benefits solely in terms of the value of the food subsidy, this indicator is not discussed further.

TABLE 4.5 *Dependence on the PDS for purchase of food grain, all States, rural areas, 1986-87 (Percentage of households by type of purchase)*

State	Type of purchase from PDS		
	No purchase from PDS	Partial purchase from PDS	All purchases from PDS
Mizoram	6.4	47.0	46.6
Kerala	12.3	79.0	8.6
Goa	20.4	69.1	10.5
Tripura	30.8	66.5	2.7
Karnataka	38.1	53.9	8.0
Andhra Pradesh	40.3	47.3	12.4
Tamil Nadu	46.5	44.9	8.5
Maharashtra	52.3	32.4	15.3
Gujarat	55.5	30.0	14.6
Meghalaya	61.2	31.5	7.4
Delhi	64.6	20.4	15.0
Sikkim	70.0	2.6	27.4
Himachal Pradesh	71.8	13.1	15.1
West Bengal	73.1	22.7	4.1
Assam	75.4	21.9	2.8
Jammu & Kashmir	76.7	10.2	13.2
Madhya Pradesh	90.9	4.8	4.3
Rajasthan	91.2	3.6	5.2
Manipur	94.6	4.5	0.9
Haryana	96.9	1.6	1.5
Uttar Pradesh	97.9	0.6	1.6
Orissa	98.3	1.2	0.5
Bihar	98.3	1.2	0.5
Punjab	99.9	0	0.1

Source Parikh (1994), Table 2

participate in PDS. To put it differently, PDS only reached around 2 per cent of the population. In Kerala, by contrast, *over 87 per cent of the population purchased grain from PDS.* Eight per cent purchased only from fair-price stores and 79 per cent purchased from PDS and the open market. Among the smaller states, participation in PDS was high in Mizoram (93.6 per cent) and Goa (79.6 per cent). In the two southern states of Andhra Pradesh and Tamil Nadu, around 55–60 per cent of the population made purchases from PDS. The picture is very similar for urban areas (Table 4.6 overleaf). While 87 per cent of the urban population in Kerala participated in PDS, 93 per cent of the population in UP and Bihar did *not* buy cereals from PDS.

TABLE 4.6 *Dependence on the PDS for purchase of food grain, all States, urban areas, 1986-87 (Percentage of households by type of purchase)*

State	Type of purchase from PDS		
	No purchase from PDS	Partial purchase from PDS	All purchases from PDS
Mizoram	1.1	54.6	44.3
Kerala	13.0	83.8	3.3
Goa Daman & Diu	18.3	70.6	11.2
Jammu & Kashmir	21.4	49.0	29.6
Delhi	26.3	17.1	56.6
Karnataka	37.3	58.9	3.8
West Bengal	40.2	51.2	8.5
Tripura	44.4	52.8	2.8
Tamil Nadu	44.6	52.8	2.7
Andhra Pradesh	48.6	47.9	3.5
Maharashtra	56.2	38.5	5.3
Assam	57.0	40.6	2.5
Meghalaya	64.1	28.6	7.3
Gujarat	68.0	24.5	7.5
Himachal Pradesh	74.7	14.1	11.3
Sikkim	79.0	5.3	15.8
Madhya Pradesh	82.6	12.1	5.3
Orissa	86.2	11.4	2.4
Haryana	92.9	4.3	2.8
Bihar	92.9	6.4	0.7
Uttar Pradesh	93.0	4.6	2.5
Rajasthan	94.4	2.2	3.4
Manipur	95.0	3.0	2.0
Punjab	95.4	3.6	1.0

Source Parikh (1994), Table 2

Two conclusions can be drawn from these findings. First, PDS is highly differentiated across states and one has to be very careful about making generalizations at the national level. Secondly, the utilization of PDS, in terms of the proportion of households purchasing PDS grain, was very low in all states of the country with the exception of Kerala, Goa and Mizoram. *The data indicate that PDS was not serving the vast majority of the country's population.*

Of all poor households, only a small fraction participated in PDS. For example, among the lowest 10 per cent of rural households in terms of expenditure, 43 per cent purchased rice from PDS, 30 per cent purchased wheat and only 10 per cent purchased jowar at the all India level (Jha 1992).[5]

Village studies
Although overall coverage is low, there is some evidence from village studies that in states as the coverage of PDS becomes more extensive, the poor buy progressively higher amounts of grain from the system. Data from village studies are important for two reasons. First, the NSS survey is now dated, and smaller studies can provide evidence for more recent years. Secondly, village studies are better at identifying the economic and social status of households and the problems that the poorer classes face in gaining access to PDS.

There is some interesting evidence from a village study that I undertook in Maharashtra in 1995–96. There are three findings of relevance from this study of Mohakal village in Pune district. First, the overall degree of participation in PDS was low. Secondly, participation or purchase from PDS was even lower among the poorest households in the village. Thirdly, PDS did not serve the rich but those among the lower and middle-income groups who could afford to make regular monthly purchases from the ration shop.

A set of village studies was undertaken recently in four states, Bihar, UP, Kerala and Andhra Pradesh, as part of a UNDP project on human development (Radhakrishna 1996). In each state, in 1994–95, three or four villages and a total of about 200 households were surveyed. The first striking result from these surveys is the total collapse of PDS in Bihar, with UP not far behind. In all the villages studied in Bihar, not one of the surveyed households reported purchases of cereals from PDS. In UP, a similar situation was recorded in three of the four villages studied. In their review of economic development over five decades in Palanpur, a village in western UP, Dreze et al. (1998) observed that the ration shop in Palanpur functioned poorly, supplying, if at all, sugar and kerosene, and was finally closed down in 1991. The Palanpur experience is 'symptomatic of the corresponding situation in rural UP as a whole' (ibid. 194). The situation was markedly different in the two southern states, which were marked by a high degree of participation in PDS. Further, the pattern of participation

---

[5] This is because the total supply of jowar in PDS is very low.

varied across expenditure classes in a progressive manner. In all but one Kerala village, households in the highest expenditure class did not buy any cereals from PDS. So the better-off households selected themselves out of PDS. A similar pattern was observed in Andhra Pradesh. In three villages, households in the highest expenditure class did not utilize PDS, in a fourth village their purchases were quite small, and only in the fifth village were there large purchases by households in this group. Note, however, that households being termed 'rich' were not very rich in absolute terms as the highest expenditure class was demarcated at a relatively low absolute level of expenditure.

To sum up, in states where PDS functioned poorly and had low coverage (such as Bihar and UP), most households, whatever their expenditure level, did not participate in PDS. In states with high coverage and an effective distribution network (such as Kerala and Andhra Pradesh), PDS was used more by the poor than by the rich.

Quantity distributed or purchased from PDS

Next we turn to the quantity of food grain purchased from fair price shops by households from different economic classes.

National Sample Survey data

Using the NSS data for 1986–87, households can be ranked by household expenditure per capita, and then the purchases by households in different expenditure fractile groups can be examined. The share of the bottom 20 per cent of all households in terms of per capita expenditure in the quantity of PDS purchases is shown in Table 4.7. In Andhra Pradesh, Kerala and Tamil Nadu, the share of food grain distributed to the lowest 20 per cent of households was close to their population share. In UP and Bihar, however, persons in the lowest 20 per cent got a disproportionately low share of cereals sold in PDS. For example, the lowest 24 per cent of the population in terms of per capita expenditure received only 14 per cent of PDS grain in the urban areas of Bihar. As PDS is a universal programme in most states, the ratio of share of food grain purchases to population share should be around one.[6] A ratio greater than one implies that a class is

[6] In other words, the poorest 20 per cent of the population should consume 20 per cent of food grain, the poorest 30 per cent should consume 30 per cent of food grain and so on.

TABLE 4.7 *Share of bottom 20 per cent of population in quantity of food grain distributed through PDS, by state and rural-urban areas, 1986-87*

State	Rural		Urban	
	% of population	% of quantity distributed	% of population	% of quantity distributed
Andhra Pradesh	26	24.6	24	28.2
Assam	24	28.4	30	33.3
Bihar	24	16.9	24	14.4
Delhi	27	56.6	26	28.1
Goa Daman & Diu	30	31.4	25	24.7
Gujarat	23	26.6	25	37.6
Haryana	24	33.2	30	21.0
Himachal Pradesh	29	21.6	31	29.4
Jammu & Kashmir	24	30.4	26	22.3
Karnataka	24	20.8	25	21.8
Kerala	25	25.1	29	28.2
Madhya Pradesh	24	20.9	24	22.9
Maharashtra	23	22.2	26	23.0
Manipur	22	21.4	26	2.4
Meghalaya	25	28.6	30	25.2
Mizoram	26	26.2	24	23.4
Orissa	21	7.1	26	6.8
Punjab	23	100.0	27	20.5
Rajasthan	24	33.3	27	36.9
Sikkim	30	25.4	32	0.0
Tamil Nadu	26	24.3	24	23.6
Tripura	26	27.0	21	25.9
Uttar Pradesh	24	10.8	27	19.0
West Bengal	23	19.3	26	23.6

Source Parikh (1994), Table 6

getting a relatively high share of food grain. The ratio was around one or greater than one for the bottom 20 per cent of the population in 15 of the 24 states surveyed (including Kerala and Andhra Pradesh).[7] In these states, the population in the bottom two deciles obtained more than a proportionate share of grain from PDS.

Another way of examining the contribution of PDS is to look at the share of purchases from the ration shop in the total amount purchased of each commodity. Consider the purchase of rice in rural areas, as reported

---

[7] This ratio is obtained by dividing the share of quantity distributed by the share of population (Parikh, 1994).

TABLE 4.8 *Share of rice purchased from the PDS in total consumption of rice in five villages of Andhra Pradesh, 1994-95 (per cent)*

Per capita expenditure category (Rs)	Village				
	Nettampadu	Singtham	Jaggasagar	Narsayapalem	Machavaram
Less than 175	31.5	24.5	31.4	52.2	25.6
175-225	30.6	41.3	16.4	21.0	22.6
225-275	17.7	0.0	10.1	24.3	19.0
275-350	0.0	0.0	0.0	8.3	13.6
All classes	30.7	26.4	22.4	22.4	26.5

Source Indrakant (1995), Table 26, page 29.

in the NSS survey of 1986–87. In Andhra Pradesh, rice purchased from PDS accounted for 39 per cent of total rice purchased by households in the lowest expenditure decile; in Madhya Pradesh, the corresponding figure was only 5 per cent (Jha 1992). So, while rice from PDS contributed substantially to total rice purchased by a very low expenditure family in Andhra Pradesh, the contribution of PDS rice to total purchases of rice was meagre in Madhya Pradesh. Secondly, in Andhra Pradesh, the share of PDS purchase in total purchase declined with a rise in the expenditure decile. This share was 39 per cent for households in the lowest expenditure decile and 21 per cent for households in the highest expenditure decile (ibid.). So while families in the highest expenditure decile also participated in PDS, the contribution of PDS rice to their total purchases was lower than the corresponding share for poorer households. In Madhya Pradesh, however, there was no similar progressive pattern of purchases, and the section of the population that bought a higher share of PDS grain than any other was the top expenditure decile.

Village studies

The UNDP-sponsored village studies in four states also have information on the quantity of grain purchased from PDS. Tables 4.8 and 4.9 show the share of rice bought from PDS in the total consumption of rice for the surveyed villages in Andhra Pradesh and Kerala. The data clearly show that poorer households depended more heavily on PDS. Summarizing the findings for Andhra Pradesh, Indrakant noted that the 'support provided by PDS to small farmers and agricultural labour households is higher than to the other classes. Further, the extent of support is more in

TABLE 4.9 *Share of rice purchased from the PDS in total consumption of rice in four villages of Kerala, 1994-95 (per cent)*

Per capita expenditure category (Rs)	Village			
	Anand	Anjengo	Edavaka	Paruthoor
Less than 175	46.0	14.4	80.3	100.0
175-225	46.5	28.9	69.6	68.1
225-275	53.0	21.2	53.9	44.8
275-350	44.5	29.5	42.4	66.5
350-500	58.4	36.8	26.6	54.2
500-1000	40.8	23.5	38.4	54.1
Above 1000	79.9	0.0	0.0	0.0
All classes	48.5	26.1	41.3	55.5

Source Radhakrishna (1996), Table 8, p. 178.

backward villages' (1995: 15) than in relatively advanced villages. In the village of Narsayapalem, for example, 52 per cent of rice consumption by the poorest households, that is, households with a per capita monthly expenditure of less than Rs 175, came from PDS rice. The corresponding share for households in the highest expenditure category (per capita expenditure of Rs 275 to 350) was 8 per cent. In the village of Nettampadu, 64.5 per cent of the total rice purchased by landless-labour households was from PDS (ibid.). At the same time, households in higher expenditure classes also purchased PDS grain. Households with a per capita expenditure of Rs 275 or Rs 300 (that is, a family income of less than Rs 1,500 a month), however, can hardly be defined as rich households. Similarly, in Kerala, in the villages of Paruthoor and Edavaka, reliance on PDS for rice consumption was very high among those in the lowest expenditure class (Table 4.10). An exception to this pattern was the village of Anand, where the share of PDS rice in total rice consumption did not fall with the level of household expenditure.

Maladministration and leakages

Several studies have documented the administrative problems with PDS and shown that in many states there is large-scale diversion of grain, wastage, low quality and unreliable provisioning.[8] Leakages could occur

---

[8] See, for example, Mooij (1999) and Ahluwalia (1993).

at two sites: at the Food Corporation of India, the nodal agency that is responsible for procurement, storage and distribution; and at the local level of administration and delivery, that is, the fair-price shop owner, ration controller, etc.

Food Corporation of India

As the budgetary food subsidy comprises the entire operational deficit of the Food Corporation of India, any waste, leakage or inefficiency in the FCI is a drain on resources. The FCI is a huge organization with branches in all parts of the country. The inefficiency and 'excessive costs of operation' of the FCI are blamed for 'spiralling government subsidies' on food, particularly by those arguing against the public control of food distribution (Sharma, Gulati and Kahkonen 1997). Let us examine this claim with data on costs from FCI performance budgets.[9]

As the FCI is responsible for buffer stock operations, the total food subsidy includes the costs associated with maintaining buffer stocks (such as handling costs, costs of storage, interest payments and administration) as well as the costs of distribution (via PDS). The total costs of storing and distributing the grain procured by the FCI are apportioned, on the basis of certain principles, to these two components of cost (that is, distribution through PDS and costs of maintaining buffer stocks).[10] The first feature of note from FCI performance budgets is that the subsidy incurred on carrying costs and on holding stocks for buffer stocking operations rose rapidly in absolute and relative terms in the 1990s. The costs associated with maintaining buffer stocks accounted for 12.3 per cent of the total cereal subsidy in 1992–93, 28 per cent the following year and 44 per cent in 1994–95. In other words, by 1994–95, the subsidy that went towards distribution to consumers was just a little over half the total subsidy on food grain. As will be shown in Chapter 6, in the 1990s, stocks held by the government have exceeded the minimum requirement significantly, and this has undoubtedly added to the costs of the FCI.

The subsidy given to the FCI is the difference between economic costs and the price obtained from sales (or sales realization). The economic cost, in turn, is defined as the sum of procurement price, procurement-

---

[9] For further details, see Swaminathan (1999).

[10] On the method of apportioning costs and anomalies therein, see BICP (1991).

related costs and distribution costs. The procurement price is the price paid by the FCI to producers for the purchase of grain. Procurement costs are the initial costs incurred during the procurement of grain at *mandis* (market yards) or other procurement centres. Distribution costs are the costs involved in storing and transporting grain to the final distribution points. The components of distribution costs are freight, handling expenses, storage charges, interest charges, transit shortages (or losses during transit), storage shortages (losses during storage) and establishment costs.

The second important feature of the change in costs in the 1990s is the growing gap between economic costs and sales realization, and this has been marked in the last two years (Table 4.10 overleaf). First, the economic costs of both rice and wheat have risen steadily during the 1990s. The economic cost of wheat rose from Rs 356.50 per quintal in 1990–91 to Rs 807.95 in 1998–99 reflecting an annual growth of 10 per cent. The economic cost of rice grew at 9.7 per cent a year over the same period, from Rs 457.52 to Rs 980.36. The average sales realization from rice and wheat did not rise as fast as their respective economic costs. In short, a growing divergence between economic costs and sales realization led to a major rise in the subsidy per unit during the 1990s.

The obvious question, then, is what led to the rise in economic costs? In the case of wheat, the most important factor was the procurement price, which grew at 11.5 per cent annually over this decade. To put it differently, the procurement price for wheat rose 145 per cent, procurement-related costs rose 71 per cent and distribution costs rose 68 per cent between 1990–91 and 1998–99. As a result, the share of procurement price in total economic cost of wheat increased, from 57 per cent in 1990–91 to 64 per cent in 1998–99 whereas the share of distribution costs in total economic costs fell correspondingly from 24.5 per cent to 19.2 per cent. In the case of rice too, procurement prices rose over this period, at an annual rate of 9.8 per cent, and the share of procurement price in total economic costs rose.

The operational costs of the FCI also rose steeply during the 1990s. The per quintal cost of distribution of wheat, for example, was Rs 92 in 1991–92 and had jumped to Rs 155 to 1998–99. If we examine the components of distribution costs, it emerges that handling expenses, storage charges, establishment charges and costs of freight were the main contributors to rising costs. Interestingly, for wheat, transport and storage

TABLE 4.10 *Economic costs and subsidy on rice and wheat, 1990–91 to 1998–99 (Rupees per quintal)*

	1990–91	1991–92	1992–93	1993–94	1994–95	1995–96	1996–97	1997–98 (RE)	1998–99 (RE)	Annual growth, 1990–98 (%)
Wheat										
Economic cost	356.5	390.79	504.1	532.03	551.17	583.95	640.16	800.5	807.95	9.99
Sales Realization	239.95	251.68	279.36	355.88	407.89	411.94	433.2	395.87	388.33	7.18
Subsidy	116.55	139.11	224.74	176.15	143.28	172.01	206.96	404.63	419.62	13.56
Rice										
Economic cost	457.52	497.04	585.27	665.1	694.71	762.82	847.69	940.4	980.36	9.73
Sales Realization	330.02	365.58	442.4	500.42	600.76	613.34	610.57	610.8	601.18	7.98
Subsidy	127.5	131.46	142.87	164.68	93.95	149.48	237.12	329.6	379.18	13.39

Note RE: Revised estimates

Source Swaminathan (1999), based on FCI Performance budgets.

TABLE 4.11 *Ratio of economic cost to procurement price for rice and wheat, 1990-91 to 1998-99*

Year	Wheat	Rice
1990-91	174.0	135.2
1991-92	185.0	133.4
1992-93	170.5	134.9
1993-94	163.5	132.9
1994-95	164.6	129.1
1995-96	166.3	131.2
1996-97	163.8	134.9
1997-98	161.0	136.9
1998-99	156.2	131.7

Source From Swaminathan (1999), based on data from the FCI.

losses declined during the 1990s. The rise in unit distribution costs was higher for rice: the per quintal cost went up from Rs 87 in 1990–91 to Rs 171 in 1998–99. Notably, the share of freight costs in total distribution costs increased sharply for rice. Clearly, this trend of rising costs of distribution is not sustainable.

Despite the rise in operational costs, surprisingly, the ratio of economic cost to procurement price declined for wheat after 1991–92 and was more or less unchanged for rice during the 1990s (Table 4.11). This ratio is an indicator of operational efficiency as it measures the costs of acquisition and distribution relative to the costs of purchase. By this criterion, operational efficiency improved in the case of wheat and showed no change in the case of rice during the 1990s.

To sum up, the increase in costs of carrying buffer stocks is one of the factors contributing to the rising total costs of the FCI. In terms of the cost component pertaining to PDS, the increase in procurement prices and not in the costs of distribution was the crucial factor in the increase in total costs of the FCI. In India's parliamentary system, the procurement price is a political decision over which the FCI has no control. The central government announces procurement prices based on the recommendations of the Commission on Agricultural Costs and Prices (CACP) that, in turn, are based on costs of production in different parts of the country. There has been tendency in recent years to announce prices that are higher than recommended prices, often due to pressures from rich farmers. This is not to deny that costs of distribution have been rising and need to be checked. It is clear that the organization and management of the FCI need restructuring so as to make it more transparent, and to lower the operational costs. However, the 'excessive costs' of the FCI are caused by factors that are conventionally outside the control of the FCI itself.

Problems of administration and corruption in delivery
Many studies of the working of PDS indicate that there are large leakages at the local level. There are many ways in which the fair-price shop owner can cheat the final consumer and I provide a few illustrations here. Food grain can be diverted from PDS by illegal sales, often accompanied by false entries in ration cards.[11] In a small survey of a tribal village, Talasari, in Thane district of Maharashtra, I found that while the people of the scheduled tribes of the village bought no sugar at all, many ration cards showed regular purchases of sugar from the ration shop (Swaminathan 1995). Another possibility is through the creation of bogus or false ration cards; Mooij (1998) describes how she found several blank application forms for the preparation of bogus cards with fair-price shop owners in Bihar. Short weighing of goods can also defraud a consumer. The quality of grain at the FCI depot and the quality of grain in the fair-price shop often differ because an intermediary or shop owner mixes the grain received with lower quality grain (with broken rice, for instance). The poor can also be cheated of their entitlement because of lack of information about when, how much, and what is available in the local fair-price shop.

In the NSS survey of 1986–87, households were asked to give reasons for not buying any (or part) of their entitlement from the ration shop for each commodity separately. The responses show that insufficient supply of goods was one of the most important reasons for not utilizing the fair-rice shop. In rural areas, in the case of rice, 25 per cent of respondents said that rice was not available and another 15 per cent said that rice was not available in sufficient quantities. In urban areas, 19 per cent said the reason for not purchasing rice was that it was not available and 22 per cent said it was not available in sufficient quantities. Thus, around 40 per cent of rural and urban respondents did not buy grain because there was none to be bought.

Although it is widely known that leakages occur, it is difficult to

---

[11] For an example of black market sales by a ration shop owner in Karnataka, see Mooij 1999: Chapter 5.

identify exactly the extent of losses, pilferage, etc. The mismatch between survey-based information on the utilization of PDS and national data on PDS sales to a state can be one indicator of the scale of leakages from PDS. Using this method, for 1986–87, the year with household survey data from the NSS, Ahluwalia estimated that only 17 per cent of the wheat lifted from the FCI by state governments reached the final consumers in Bihar (Ahluwalia 1993). Leakages were also markedly high in Assam and Orissa (ibid.).

It is obvious to any person with experience of PDS that the problems of corruption, misuse, and mismanagement of the public delivery system are very serious, and responsible for undermining the institution in many parts of the country. Ultimately, such institutions will only function and deliver if they are accountable to the people and if there is public demand for a PDS and public involvement in monitoring it.

Impact on prices

One of the objectives of PDS and the system of food management in India has been to keep the prices of basic goods under control. In the 1970s and 80s, the real price of rice and wheat declined, indicating that the objective of providing cheap food was met (Bhalla 1994). When, for example, the index of wheat prices was deflated by the index of wholesale prices, the real price (or relative price) of wheat fell steadily through the 1970s and 80s. If this ratio is set at 100 in 1970–71, it had fallen to 65.2 for wheat and 78.9 for rice in 1991–92 (Bhalla 1994: Table 8, p 152). In the 1990s, however, this tendency towards a decline in the real price of food was reversed, particularly for rice. From 1991–92, as shown in Table 4.12 (overleaf), the real price of rice has risen steadily and reached 111 in 1997–98 (when indexed at 100 in 1981–82). Wheat prices remained relatively low until the mid-1990s but even here, the relative price has shown a tendency to rise in the last few years. Since the decline in relative price in the 1970s was steep, the real price of food in the 1990s is probably still lower than that in 1970. Nevertheless, it is of serious concern that a major achievement of food policy in India – the lowering of the real price of food – has begun to be reversed in the 1990s.

Not only did the wholesale price of food increase at a relatively rapid rate in the early 1990s but even the prices of food grain sold through PDS rose sharply. Figures 6.3 to 6.6 show the dramatic rise in issue prices from

TABLE 4.12 *Index of real price of rice and wheat, 1981–82 to 1997–98 (1981–82=100)*

Year	Wholesale price index for			Relative price index for	
	Rice	Wheat	All commodities	Rice	Wheat
1981–82	100	100	100.0	100	100
1982–83	115	111	104.9	110	106
1983–84	129	114	112.8	114	101
1984–85	121	111	120.1	101	92
1985–86	127	119	125.4	101	95
1986–87	134	127	132.7	101	96
1987–88	146	135	143.6	102	94
1988–89	161	154	154.3	104	100
1989–90	169	148	165.7	102	89
1990–91	178	172	182.7	97	94
1991–92	217	204	207.8	104	98
1992–93	249	227	228.7	109	99
1993–94	266	253	247.8	107	102
1994–95	294	273	274.7	107	99
1995–96	316	271	295.8	107	92
1996–97	347	330	314.6	110	105
1997–98	365	333	329.8	111	101

Notes   The whole sale price indices are average of weeks.
The relative price index is the price index for wheat/rice divided by the all commodity price index.
Source   *Economic Survey,* different years.

the late 1980s through the early 1990s. Between 1990 and 1994, the central issue price of the common variety of rice rose 85.8 per cent and that of wheat rose 71.8 per cent (Table 4.13). During the same period, the Index of Wholesale prices rose 44.4 per cent. Between 1990–91 and 1994–95, the Consumer Price Index for Agricultural Labourers (CPIAL) rose 53 per cent. In other words, the cumulative increase in prices of food grain sold in PDS was higher than the increase in general price indices. The cumulative price increase was higher for rice of low quality, the common variety, than for rice of high quality, the superfine variety.

By contrast, in the 1970s and 1980s, the inflation in food prices was moderate in relation to inflation in general prices. Between 1970–71 and 1980–81, the Index of Wholesale Prices for food grain rose 116 per cent, the general Index of Wholesale Prices rose 157 per cent, the CPIAL rose 105 per cent and the prices of rice and wheat in PDS rose 65 and 86 per cent respectively. In other words, the rate of increase in central issue prices was lower than in all the other major price indices. Between 1980–81 and

TABLE 4.13 *Central issue prices of rice and wheat, 1990 to 1999 (Rupees per quintal)*

Date when prices	Rice			Wheat
effective	Common	Fine	Superfine	
June 1990	289	349	370	234
Dec. 1991	377	437	458	280
Jan. 1993	437	497	518	330
Feb. 1994	537	617	648	402
June 1997				
(i) BPL	350	350	–	250
(ii) APL	550	650	750#	450
February 1999*	700	–	905#	650
(ii) APL				
April 1999*	700	–	905#	682
(ii) APL				

Notes * A hike in BPL prices was announced and then revoked.

\# From December 1995, rice is classified into two groups: common and grade A quality. The average price for Grade A rice (fine and superfine varieties) was Rs 700 in 1997 and was raised to Rs 905 in 1999.

Source Economic Survey, different years.

1990, the increase in issue prices remained lower than that in the Wholesale Price Index and the CPIAL though the difference was narrower. In the early 1990s, specifically between 1990 and 1994, as mentioned above, the pattern was reversed with issue prices rising much faster than other price indices.

Price fluctuations are harmful to poor consumers, and stabilizing prices has been another objective of food policy. Evidence shows that seasonal and regional variations in rice and wheat prices have been lowered. First, comparative price data show that domestic prices of rice and wheat have been more stable than international prices (Pal, Bahl and Mruthyunjaya 1993).[12] Secondly, the coefficient of variation in the prices of rice and wheat is lower than the variation in production and market arrivals of these crops (ibid.). While overall fluctuations have been kept in check, there has been an increase in domestic prices in years of major shortfall, such as in 1973 and 1980 for rice. Thirdly, seasonal variations in prices have been low in relation to fluctuations in output for both commodities (ibid.).

---

[12] See, also, Bhalla 1994 and Nayyar and Sen 1994.

To sum up, one of the key objectives of PDS and food policy in India has been to keep the price of basic commodities in check, and to make food available at reasonable prices to consumers in all parts of the country. While the real price of food was steadily lowered in the 1970s and 80s, and price fluctuations were also low, there was a reversal of this trend in the 1990s, with a steep rise in the price of food items. Inflation in food prices, of course, hurts the poor the most as they spend a large share of their total budget on food.

The Kerala experience

Kerala, as is evident, is the only state in India with a successful PDS and with a near-universal coverage by PDS. Kerala is in a class of its own both in terms of participation in PDS and in terms of the quantity of food grain distributed. Delivery of food grain would have to increase substantially if other states were to follow the Kerala example and provide a reasonable quantity of food grain through fair-price shops. *Kerala's experience shows that with political commitment, food and nutrition security can be enhanced through an effective system of public distribution of food.*

The establishment of an effective PDS in Kerala was the outcome of a strong people's movement for food.[13] Ration shops were first set up during 1942–43 in response to a food crisis. In Malabar and Travancore, two of the three constituents of the state of Kerala, 'the public distribution system was directly the consequence of mass action and government response to such action during the period of the food crisis' (Ramachandran 1996: 245). In Malabar, for instance, as E.M.S. Namboodiripad stated in an interview a few years ago, '*kisan sabhas* [peasant organizations], trade unions and other mass organizations, insisted on procurement from landlords and distribution through fair price shops. Because of our pressure, and because of the administrative need of the British Government itself, they set up ration shops' (Ramachandran 1998). As the newspaper accounts compiled by K.G. Sivaswamy show, there was tremendous public demand for rationing in Malabar and in response, rationing was introduced in selected towns, and later extended to rural areas (Sivaswamy 1946). Malabar was, in fact, the first region in the country in which rural rationing

---

[13] I have drawn heavily on Ramachandran 1996 in this section.

was introduced. In Travancore, there were active struggles for the provision of rations by coir worker's union.

After the War, PDS survived due to pressure from people's organizations for its continuation. With the formation of the state of Kerala in 1957, the first Communist ministry took up the task of providing an effective system of delivery of food grain throughout the state. Again, in 1964, during an acute shortage of food in Kerala, political demands for rationing led to a further expansion of the system of fair-price shops. The food question became an important political issue and was, in fact, one of the central issues in the run-up to the elections of 1967 (Mooij 1999). One of the first acts of the new Communist-led ministry was to approach the centre with a demand for a raised allocation of food grain in order to expand the ration scale. The demand for food and, specifically, for distribution of cheap grain through fair-price shops, was an important political demand raised by the Left in Kerala, and even the Congress (I) government at the Centre agreed to support the policies and demands of the government in Kerala. The political demand for food, reflected in mass protests and struggles, was thus critical in establishing and strengthening PDS.

Let me turn to some of the main features of PDS in Kerala. The first striking feature of PDS in Kerala is that its coverage is almost universal. All households that do not have land holdings sufficient to produce food grain for their own consumption are eligible for a ration card. In 1991, around 95 per cent of all households were covered by PDS and possessed a ration card (Kannan 1995). PDS effectively reaches rural households (unlike in states such as Maharashtra where there is a strong urban bias) *and* urban households *and* poor households.

Secondly, the monthly entitlement of food grain per adult is 13.8 kg. in Kerala (or 460 grams per day) as compared to 10 kg. in Maharashtra and 8 kg. in Bihar. The Kerala scale satisfies the minimum requirement of 370 gms of cereals per person per day recommended by the Indian Council of Medical Research (ICMR, 1990). In other words, unlike in many other states, the current entitlement or ration scale in Kerala is adequate in relation to minimum cereal requirements. To be credible and effective, PDS must provide a minimum quantity of food grain.[14]

---

[14] Venugopal 1992 makes a similar comment.

Thirdly, the quantity of food grain purchased from PDS, as has been noted earlier, is high, higher than in most other states, and makes a significant contribution to household nutrition. In 1991, the annual offtake of food grain from PDS averaged 69.6 kg. per person in Kerala. In the same year, the annual per capita supply of food grain from PDS was 5 kg. in Punjab, 7 kg. in UP, 9 kg. in Madhya Pradesh, 23 kg. in West Bengal and 35 kg. in Andhra Pradesh (Table 4.4).

Fourthly, while the scheme is universal, there is evidence to show that the system is progressive and that the poor depend relatively more on PDS than the rich. A sample survey of consumers conducted as early as 1977 found that families with an annual income less than Rs 3,600 received 87 per cent of the food grain sold in PDS and accounted for 59 per cent of the total population (George 1979). Further, for households in the lowest income category (of Rs 600 per annum), purchases from PDS accounted for 18 per cent of total calories consumed (ibid.). Ten years later, a representative survey conducted in 1987 found a clear negative association between household income and utilization of PDS (Koshy et al. 1989). In the lowest income category, that is, households with a monthly income of less than Rs 100, rice purchased from PDS accounted for 40 per cent of total rice consumption. At the other end of the income scale, for households with a monthly income greater than Rs 3,000, rice from PDS accounted for only 3 per cent of total consumption. Also, households with incomes of less than Rs 100 a month bought 71 per cent of the rice that they were eligible to buy. Households with more than Rs 3,000 a month only bought 6 per cent of their entitlement. Furthermore, of all users of PDS, the majority belonged to the lower income brackets, and only 5 per cent comprised households with a monthly income greater than Rs 1,000. Another interesting finding of this survey was that low-income consumers said that they did not face problems in terms of availability or quality.

Fifthly, the functioning of ration shops and the delivery system is much better than in other parts of the country and this is reflected in responses obtained from consumers. Summarizing the findings of the state-wide survey undertaken by Koshy and others, Ramachandran noted that 'low-income consumers did not have serious complaints regarding rice quality and did not complain that ration shops were overcrowded; 70 per cent of respondents did not have serious complaints about weights and measures used in the shops, and 96 per cent said that there was no problem of availability with respect to rice and wheat' (Ramachandran 1996: 250). However, 'all respondents wanted the range of commodities available through the system to be extended' (ibid.)

Lastly, PDS, given its scale and scope, has caused a real improvement in consumption and nutrition. A small but detailed study conducted in the mid-1970s showed that the rice subsidy had a significant and positive impact on all indicators of dietary quality and nutrition including calories per adult, proteins per adult, and child nutritional status (Kumar 1979). Further, an incremental rice subsidy had 6–10 times the impact of an increment to total household income on indicators of nutrition (ibid.). As mentioned above, the annual purchase of grain from PDS in Kerala provides about one-half of the cereal requirements of a person.

Concluding remarks

This chapter showed that there are huge inter-state variations in the working of the public distribution system in India, with the southern states led by Kerala having the most effective and extensive system both in terms of coverage or participation and in terms of quantity of food grain distributed. The overall finding from the survey conducted by the NSS in 1986–87 was that of low participation in PDS: in several states including Bihar, Madhya Pradesh, Orissa, Rajasthan, and UP, less than 10 per cent of households bought grain from PDS. Turning to quantities, in 1995, the annual average per capita offtake of food grain from PDS was less than 3 kg. in UP and Bihar, 10 kg. in Maharashtra, 33 kg. in Andhra Pradesh and 53 kg. in Kerala. Although inter-state differences have persisted over many years, there have also been changes over time. In the 1980s, for example, there was a major increase in offtake in Andhra Pradesh and Kerala and further decline in offtake, from an already low level, in Bihar. At the aggregate level, the offtake from PDS declined after 1991–92. Between 1991 and 1998, per capita offtake declined in the majority of states. More recently, with the introduction of Targeted PDS, the pattern of distribution across states has, again, altered.

There has been heated debate about the extent of urban bias in PDS. The more important question, however, is the extent to which the poor have access to PDS. On this issue, we examined the results of the survey undertaken by the NSS in 1986–87 as well as a range of village studies. Our analysis showed that in states with high coverage and an effective distribution network (such as Kerala and Andhra Pradesh) the poor had greater access to PDS. In states with an inefficient and ineffective distribution network (such as UP and Bihar), PDS reached neither the poor nor the rich.

In the 1990s, the weakening of PDS has shown up in the high inflation in food prices. After a decline for over two decades, there was a sharp rise in the relative price of rice, and to a lesser extent wheat, in the 1990s. Inflation in the prices of PDS food grain has exceeded inflation in other price and cost of living indices. Since the late 1980s, the issue prices of grain in PDS have risen rapidly. One of the main objectives of food policy, namely to keep food prices low and affordable, has thus been undermined in recent years.

Another major problem with PDS is the scale of corruption and leakage from the system. The continuing rise in operational costs of the FCI, the organization responsible for procurement, storage and distribution, is a worrying phenomenon. However, I argued that the major factor in the rise in costs was the rise in procurement prices, a variable outside the control of the FCI. Nevertheless, there is need to check the rise in operational costs and reorient procurement policy, and this is taken up in Chapter 7. Malpractices are also widely prevalent at all levels of administration of the delivery system in many parts of the country, and this problem has to be attended to by means of political and administrative reforms.

Lastly, the discussion of the Kerala experience showed that it is possible to provide minimum nutritional support to almost the entire population through a well-run network of fair-price shops. In Kerala, PDS reaches almost the entire population. There is a good network of well-administered fair-price shops that is accessible to the poor. On average, the quantity of food grain distributed per person meets roughly half the nutritional requirements though low-income households depend more on PDS than high-income households do.

In conclusion, this chapter has given ample evidence of large differences in the coverage and functioning of PDS across states. This is not surprising, given the differences in the class character and politics of different state governments. Even though some parameters of food distribution are determined by the central government, state governments make final decisions on policy (including on quantities, prices and coverage) and are responsible for implementation. The diverse experience of states and the relative success of Kerala show that strong political support is essential to establish and maintain an effective system of food security. It also points to differences in the quality of governance, and the importance of government commitment to the effective provision of public goods and services such as through PDS. Given that PDS has failed in large parts of the country, the task ahead is it to restructure it so as to make it an effective tool of food security.

five

Structural Adjustment and Food Subsidy

Selected Country Experiences

In the theory and experience of orthodox structural adjustment, reducing subsidies – including food subsidies – has been an important way of reducing public expenditure. In a chapter of *Adjustment with a Human Face*, Pinstrup-Andersen, et al. observed that 'capping or reducing food subsidies was part of about one-third of 94 adjustment programmes supported by the IMF during recent years' (Cornia, Jolly and Stewart 1991: 83). In another study of World Bank adjustment lending, it was noted that 'food price subsidies are a favourite target in adjustment' (Pinstrup-Andersen and Pandya-Lorch 1994: 487). Specifically, structural adjustment has entailed a reduction in food subsidies and a shift from universal to targeted schemes in many countries. One of the means of reducing the food subsidy bill has been the introduction of food stamps or coupons. This chapter attempts to provide a concise account of the impact of structural adjustment on food subsidies and food security in Mexico, Sri Lanka, Jamaica, Zambia and Tunisia, focussing on the effects of policy changes on food consumption and nutrition among the poor. The choice of these countries is based on the fact that in all cases food subsidy programmes underwent major changes in the course of structural adjustment, and all but Tunisia shifted to a targeted system of food stamps.

Mexico

The case of Mexico, one of the first countries to be hit by the debt crisis of the 1980s, shows clearly how budgetary pressures changed food subsidy policy. Policy changes in the 1980s were guided primarily by the objective of expenditure reduction. The government wished to reduce food subsidies, and to do so, it shifted from general to targeted schemes. CONASUPO or the National Basic Foods Company was the state enterprise that undertook the import, processing and distribution of subsidized foods through a national chain of stores. The operational deficit of CONASUPO increased between 1965 and 1982 (the start of the debt crisis), although it never exceeded 1.4 per cent of GDP and the average over the period was less than 0.5 per cent of GDP. The major policy changes after 1982 included the elimination of the public programme (termed SAM) aimed at raising domestic grain production and consumption, a shift from general to targeted subsidies and a trimming down of CONASUPO from being a food redistributive agency to a grain importing agency (Brachet-Marquez and Sherraden 1994). General price subsidies on a range of commodities, including bread, tortillas, beans, eggs, milk and cooking oil, were reduced during the 1980s and eventually replaced by a targeted subsidy on tortillas and milk. The general subsidy on grain and oil provided by CONASUPO fell by 20 per cent in 1984 and by 50 per cent in 1985 and 1986. There was a small reversal in 1988 and 1989 on account of the Economic Solidarity Pact (a social contract that regulated wages and prices). On the whole, between 1982 and 1988, food subsidies were cut by 80 per cent.

In April 1986, a targeted food stamps programme was started and this provided *tortibonos* (tortilla stamps) that could be exchanged for tortillas at subsidized prices. There were three types of targeting involved. First, there was an income criterion whereby only households with an income less than twice the minimum wage were eligible for food stamps. Secondly, there was geographic targeting as only low-income neighbourhoods had retail stores where subsidized food could be purchased. Thirdly, there was an element of self-targeting as households had to go and register at local CONASUPO offices for tortilla stamps. In 1991, a new scheme called *tortivales* was introduced in urban areas. The programme was means-tested and around 2.8 million families in urban areas participated in the programme in the mid-1990s. Households eligible for the scheme were given an electronic card that could be used to obtain 1 kg. of free tortillas a day from specified private retail stores. Designated banks reimbursed the shop-owners once a week. More recently, a pilot scheme based on cash transfers has been started with, perhaps, the ultimate objective of switching from food to cash subsidies (Appendini 1997).

These changes in food policy affected many households adversely. First, targeting led to a fall in the number of households that received subsidized food. The number of families buying from CONASUPO declined by over 80 per cent between 1983 and 1987. The two major subsidy schemes of the 1990s, *tortivales* and the milk subsidy, were both urban-based programmes, and little attention was paid to poor rural consumers. Thus, with the introduction of targeting, substantial sections of the population that faced falling incomes did not have access to subsidized food.

Secondly, in a period of falling wages and incomes, households had to bear sharp rises in prices of basic food commodities. The price of tortillas increased by 140 per cent between 1982 and 1988. During the same period, per capita GDP declined by 15 per cent. Most general price subsidies were on goods that were a larger proportion of the diets of the poor than of the rich. The elimination of these subsidies without an adequate increase in targeted programmes affected the poor adversely (Lustig 1992). The cost of buying a basic minimum basket of food increased rapidly relative to wages at a time when minimum wages were declining. In 1982, the cost of a basic food basket was 30 per cent of the minimum wage; it rose to 50 per cent in 1986 and 125 per cent in 1990.

Thirdly, there was a fall in consumption during the major part of the 1980s. A survey undertaken by the National Consumers Institute in Mexico City showed that the 'majority of families with incomes lower than twice the minimum wage experienced a decrease in consumption of all food products except tortillas' (ibid.). Between 1980 and 1988, per capita consumption of corn fell from 239 kg. to 142 kg., per capita wheat consumption fell from 53 kg. to 49 kg. and per capita bean consumption fell from 20 kg. to 14 kg. Milk consumption increased a little but around 40 per cent of the population did not consume milk regularly. The composition of diets changed – there was a decline in the consumption of animal protein (beef, pork and eggs) and a shift towards a less nutritious diet.

Sri Lanka

Sri Lanka has been at the centre of discussion in the debate on development strategies for having achieved high levels of 'human development' at low levels of income. In the realm of policies of food security, there are two striking features of the Sri Lankan experience over the last fifty years. For more than thirty years, Sri Lanka had an effective and universal system of food rationing, one that provided heavily subsidized food. As in India, food rationing was first introduced in Sri Lanka in 1942 as a war-time relief measure.[1] Initially, the quota varied by age but from 1954 onwards a uniform quota of four pounds (or two measures) of rice per person per week was introduced. In other words, the entitlement for an individual was about 7.2 kg. of rice each month. The price of ration rice changed from time to time but was highly subsidized. From 1960 to 1966, for example, both measures of rice were priced at Rs 0.25 a measure. From 1966, the quota was halved to one measure and this was provided free. In 1970, the system went back to two measures a week with the first measure being free and the second measure being priced at Rs 0.75. In 1972 for the first time, a distinction was made between persons paying income tax and those not paying income tax. The latter received one measure free whereas the former had to pay for both measures. In 1977, the scheme provided 2 measures a week at Rs 2.00 a measure for income tax payers. For those not paying tax, the first pound (half a measure) was free and the remaining 3 pounds could be purchased at Rs 2.00.

Faced with a large budget deficit and inflation, in 1977, a newly elected Sri Lankan government, following negotiations with the IMF, decided to cut food subsidies. It is telling that the IMF side wanted to 'eliminate food subsidies *totally*' whereas domestic policy makers tried to maintain a food subsidy for the bottom 40 per cent of the population (Jayawardena et al. 1988: 15, emphasis in original). Thus, in 1978, the policy changed from a universal ration to a means-tested or targeted ration whereby only households with a monthly income less than Rs 300 were eligible for the ration. Next, in 1979, there was a shift to a targeted food stamp programme. Families with a monthly income less than Rs 300 were eligible for food stamps and families with an income of between Rs 300 and Rs 750 were also eligible for some stamps (depending on household

---

[1] This account draws heavily on Anand and Kanbur (1991).

size and composition). The stamps could be used to purchase a specified basket of commodities (including rice, paddy, wheat flour, bread, sugar and powdered milk) (see Edirisinghe 1988). Lastly, under the agreement with the IMF, the administered prices of various commodities were raised in 1980, leading to a rise in the prices of rice, flour, sugar, etc.

What were the consequences of the new policies? First, the number of beneficiary households declined significantly. When targeted rations were introduced in 1978, the number of participating households fell to 7.6 million persons, that is, by about 50 per cent. The shift from universal to targeted transfers was associated with an increased likelihood of excluding the very poor and needy from the programme. If households are categorized by per capita income, in the lowest income quintile, 76 per cent of households received food stamps in 1982 (Edirisinghe 1987). In the second lowest income quintile, 63 per cent of households received food stamps whereas 14.5 per cent of households in the top income quintile received food stamps. In other words, although the recipients in upper income groups were reduced, a significant proportion of households in the lower income groups was also excluded from the food stamp programme.

Secondly, as the value of food stamps was fixed in nominal terms, the real value of the subsidy declined with inflation. At 1959 prices, the per capita food subsidy was Rs 62.29 in 1979 and it fell to about a third of its value, Rs 20.72, by 1982 (Anand and Kanbur 1991). As a consequence, the contribution of the food subsidy to total expenditure fell. In the lowest expenditure quintile, for example, the rice ration accounted for 26 per cent of total expenditure in 1978–79 whereas the food stamps accounted for only 15 per cent of total expenditure in 1981–82 (Edirisinghe 1987).

Thirdly, with the removal of subsidies and devaluation, prices of several food commodities rose sharply. The index of food prices (with 1952=100) went up from 203 in 1977 to 263 in 1979, 450 in 1982 and 611 in 1984 (Herring 1987). The prices of most major food commodities doubled between 1979 and 1982. The price of wheat flour, for example, rose by 170 per cent, while that of sugar rose by 133 per cent over these three years (Edirisinghe 1988).

Fourthly, the shift from a universal ration to means-tested and non-indexed food stamps adversely affected consumption and nutrition among the poor. In an evaluation of the scheme, the Ministry of Plan Implementation recognized that the new programme 'put more families at risk nutritionally than did the old ration system' (Herring 1987: 174–75). Several studies show that there was a decline in per capita calorie intake for persons in the lowest three deciles of the population (Anand and Harris 1990). Anthropometric data from two surveys of nutritional status, under-taken in 1975–76 and 1980–82, that is, prior to targeting and after targeting, showed an increase in the proportion of children suffering from acute malnutrition (Sahn 1987).

The experience of Sri Lanka shows that the food subsidy played a role in maintaining certain nutritional levels and that the sharp decline in food subsidy in the late 1970s adversely affected nutrition. In particular, 'the burden of real cuts in the food subsidy budget is likely to have fallen disproportionately on the poor' (Anand and Kanbur 1991: 80).

Zambia

Two phases can be demarcated in the growth of the Zambian economy after Independence (Mwanza et al. 1992). The first phase, from 1964 to 1974, was a period when the economy prospered as the price of its main product and export commodity, copper, rose. This was a period of rising profits and rising government revenues. During the second phase, from 1974 through to the 1990s, the economy faltered and fell into a deep debt crisis as copper prices fell and terms of trade worsened. By 1989, Zambia had a debt to export ratio of 516 per cent and a debt to GDP ratio of 136 per cent. During the 1980s and 90s, several adjustment programmes were introduced with the support of the IMF and World Bank.[2] In 1987, there was a break with the IMF and Zambia followed an independent develop-ment strategy. Eventually, the country could not do without foreign funds and returned to the IMF fold.

During adjustment, there were attempts to reduce the food subsidy for maize meal. Maize is the most important agricultural commodity in Zambia, accounting for about 70 per cent of the marketed value of all agricultural commodities. Subsidy policies have been geared both towards producers as well as urban consumers. There have been producer subsidies for maize, particularly for those in remote or outlying areas. Consumer prices were kept in control by means of controls over marketing and sale

---

[2] For a chronology of the main IMF agreements, see Jones (1994).

to millers. The extent of consumer subsidy as a per cent of the actual retail price varied from year to year, and peaked at 72 per cent in 1977 (Kumar 1988). The extent of subsidy fell in the early 1980s and rose again to around 59 per cent in 1986 (ibid.).

Until the 1980s, the marketing of maize was controlled by a parastatal organization, the National Agricultural Marketing Board, and the price of breakfast meal was kept low. The price of breakfast meal increased at about two-thirds the rate of general inflation. In 1986, however, the government attempted to differentiate between prices of two types of maize meal, breakfast meal and the more inferior roller meal. The government announced a doubling in the price of breakfast meal while keeping the price of roller meal unchanged. This led to a sudden demand for roller meal. As millers were not clear about how the subsidy on roller meal was going to be reimbursed, they stopped production and shortages developed. Overnight, both roller meal and breakfast meal became unavailable or unaffordable. This sparked off extensive rioting and looting and resulted in deaths as well. The food riots led to a reversal of the price hike and to the nationalization of thirteen large private mills. The adjustment and fall in incomes had led a large number of poor consumers to shift from high quality foods to maize meal, the only commodity with a stable price. In this context, the announcement of a price rise for maize created large-scale rioting.

The next major change in food subsidies occurred in January 1989 when the government introduced a system of food coupons. Coupons were made available to all urban households but not to rural households. Eligible households received a fixed amount of coupons that varied with the number of household members. Coupons were issued monthly and could be used to purchase either type of maize meal at government retail stores or registered private stores. Retailers in turn could reimburse the coupons at post office branches. In July 1989, targeting of coupons on the basis of incomes was begun. All employees in the formal sector had to state their income and only households with an annual income less than K 20,500 (or US $ 1,300) were eligible for coupons. All households with incomes from the informal sector were eligible for coupons but the number of dependants was limited to six.

What were the effects of the introduction of food coupons? First, the food stamp scheme had the intended impact on government expenditures, namely a reduction in the food subsidy bill. Budgetary costs fell to about a third of the previous level. Secondly, although changes in coverage are difficult to assess, many poor households were excluded from the new scheme. Based on interviews with persons from various institutions, Richard Pearce found that 'a significant minority of vulnerable households are not able to use the system' (Pearce 1991: 444). Households could register, for example, only in the first two months of the scheme and those who were left out had no way of being included later. It was also difficult to make changes in registration when changes in family size occurred. In many areas, private traders were not interested in participating in the scheme and, as a result, access to subsidized food was not easy for some households, particularly those living in low-income districts. Thus, food security worsened among 'resource-poor rural households, many of whom are headed by women' (Pearce 1994: 96). Thirdly, the real value of the subsidy declined. As Pearce observes, 'the cost of minimum household expenditures on maize far outstripped the general rate of price increase' (Pearce 1991: 444). The estimated expenditure on maize for an average family of 6 persons requiring about 50 kg. of maize meal increased 417 per cent between 1988 and 1991.

Jamaica

Jamaica is a country that is often cited as an example of a low-income country that has achieved high levels of human development. The outstanding health record as well as improvement in nutritional status during the period 1960 to 1985 was clearly associated with widespread public support (Dreze and Sen 1989). Following an economic recession, in 1977, structural adjustment was initiated when the first standby agreement with the IMF was signed. Since then, there have been more than ten IMF agreements and three World Bank structural adjustment programmes (Handa and King 1997). With the defeat of the People's National Party and a change in government in 1980, the pace of liberalization quickened. A reduction in food subsidies and social sector expenditure in general was one component of adjustment in the 1980s. Between 1983 and 1986 alone, real current expenditure on social sectors fell by 40 per cent (Grosh 1992). These changes to the system of food subsidies occurred in a period of economic recession.

Up to 1984, there was a system of generalized price subsidies on several food commodities (including corn meal, wheat flour and skimmed powder milk). In 1984, general subsidies were eliminated and replaced by a targeted food stamp and an additional school-feeding programme. Some general subsidies were reintroduced in 1986–88 and then phased out. There were two target groups for the food stamp programme. First, a group of vulnerable individuals was to be covered, and this category included pregnant or lactating women, children under five, and elderly, poor or disabled persons receiving Poor Relief. Secondly, a means-tested approach was used to identify households eligible for food stamps. The benchmark used for eligibility was an annual income of J $ 2600 (or US $ 475).[3] This was lower than the cut-off used by the Statistical Institute of Jamaica to identify the lowest income group (J $ 3000). Food stamps were to be issued on a bi-monthly basis and the value of stamps was different for the varied categories of eligible individuals.[4]

What have been the effects of the shift from general subsidies to targeted food stamps? First, with a shift to food stamps, a reduction in government spending on food subsidies was indeed achieved. Between 1972 and 1975, about 1 per cent of national income was spent on food subsidies (Boyd 1988). To protect households from the fall in wages and rise in poverty in the late 1970s, spending on food subsidies was increased, and it went up to 6 per cent of national income in 1977 (ibid.). By 1994, however, spending on food stamps had fallen to 0.23 per cent of GDP.[5] In the early 1990s, with high inflation, the expenditure on food stamps fell sharply. Total spending in 1994 was only 57 per cent of the expenditure of 1991 in real terms.

Secondly, within a year of their introduction, the real value of stamps fell by 17 per cent (ibid.). Although the value of food stamps was revised later, the revaluation did not keep pace with inflation and the real value of the stamps was eroded over time. Between 1990 and 1993, for instance, the total value of stamps was raised by 100 per cent but the general

---

[3] The poverty line was revised upwards in 1989.
[4] For example, in 1992, pregnant and lactating women received coupons worth J $ 45 as did children below the age of six. Elderly persons received J $ 60 of coupons as did single person households and poor families received J $ 105 every two months.
[5] This excludes spending on the school feeding programme but even with that the total spending on food programmes would be much lower than in the 1970s.

consumer price index increased by 226 per cent and the price index for food and drink items increased by 232 per cent.

Thirdly, high inflation in food prices led to a steep rise in the cost of a minimum basket of commodities. In October 1984, for example, the minimum cost of a basket of commodities for the survival of a family of five was estimated to be J $ 120 per week. By contrast, the minimum wage was only J $ 40 a week. So even if two members of a five-member family earned the minimum wage, they would be able to buy only 50 per cent of the minimum basket even if they spent 75 per cent of the earnings on food (ibid.). As many of the basic staples were imported, devaluation raised their prices significantly. The price of imported food rose sharply, and these were often high-calorie foods. In addition, as the price of basic food items rose, the quality of food deteriorated (ibid.).

Fourthly, the number of participants in the food stamp programme was restricted. Initially, the programme began by distributing stamps to 142,000 persons in 1984. The number of recipients varied from year to year. Although the goal had been to reach 400,000 beneficiaries or about 18 per cent of the population, there were only 270,000 recipients in 1995. So almost ten years after the programme began, only 67 per cent of the goal had been achieved.

Fifthly, targeting has led to under-coverage or the exclusion of eligible persons. The identification of 'poor' households was based on a crude and simple survey with no attempts to verify reported incomes except through observing the 'quality of housing and consumer goods ... during a brief home visit' (Grosh 1992: 27). More importantly, perhaps, there was no system of continuous verification or re-registration. After the first round in 1984, subsequent re-registrations were only undertaken in 1987 and then 1989. Participation was also constrained by the fact that beneficiaries had personally to collect the stamps on certain days of the month. Altogether, the new targeted system of coupons left out many of the poorest. A study conducted in 1988 found that 53 per cent of households in the poorest quintile were not receiving food stamps (ibid.). Households in this quintile are all eligible for food stamps as the family income falls below the specified amount of J $ 2600. In other words, the majority of eligible households were not receiving food stamps. Secondly, of all households with pregnant or lactating women, 63 per cent were excluded. Thirdly, only about half of the households with malnourished children received food stamps. Fourthly, in the poorest quintile of households with elderly persons, 45 per cent were excluded from food stamps. Thus, a large and significant proportion of eligible persons and households were excluded from the system of food stamps.

Finally, the data available, though limited, indicate a worsening in nutritional outcomes in the early 1980s. Data from two surveys of children between the ages of 0 and 4 conducted in 1978 and 1985 show that the percentage of malnourished children increased from 38 to 41 per cent between these years (Boyd 1988). The worsening occurred in both rural and urban areas. This conclusion is also supported by evidence from hospital data. These data show that the proportion of malnourished children admitted to hospital rose between 1978 and 1981, then fell slightly, and rose again in 1984 and 1985 (ibid.). The evidence on consumption expenditures, food share and income poverty indicates that there was a worsening in living standards between 1989 and 1992 (this was followed by a significant improvement in 1993 although it remains to be seen whether the turnaround in 1993 is sustained: Handa and King 1997).

Tunisia

By 1980, Tunisia had graduated to the category of middle income countries and was 'considered a model of successful development' (Radwan et al. 1991: 1). There was boom during the decade 1972–82, driven by the growth of foreign exchange, primarily from worker remittances, tourism and oil revenues. These resources were used by the state to promote modern agricultural growth and industrialization. From 1983, however, a crisis in the current account of the balance of payments developed and the burden of debt service rose. In response, orthodox stabilization and structural adjustment measures were introduced from 1986 onwards. As part of these reforms, a reduction of subsidies, including food subsidies, was attempted. The first attempt to increase the price of foods was in December 1983 when a doubling of prices of cereal products was announced. There were widespread and spontaneous protests in all parts of the country, starting among peasants, and the unemployed and students in poor towns in the south. A week later, in response to the 'bread riots', the President rescinded the price increase. In the early 1990s, as part of a structural adjustment loan, a different approach was taken, one based on self-targeting and this policy reduced expenditure on food subsidies.

Let me begin by describing the system of food subsidies that was prevalent in the 1970s and 1980s.[6] Tunisia operated a system of generalized price subsidies on a range of basic food commodities. The system was universal and run by the Caisse Generale de Compensation (CGC). Since there were no quantity restrictions, benefits were proportional to consumption. The subsidized commodities included cereals such as wheat and durum wheat, cooking oil, sugar, milk and meat. In the case of cereals, the price subsidy was introduced at the processing stage: millers sold their products at government-fixed prices and were compensated in turn. Wheat was processed into baking flour and pastry flour and durum wheat was converted into semolina and used to prepare couscous and pasta. Bakeries bought the subsidized wheat flour and produced two types of bread (gros pain and baguette) that were sold at fixed prices.

By the 1990s, the World Bank and other proponents of structural adjustment decided that the general price subsidies were 'costly and inefficient' because they 'claimed a large and unsustainable share of government resources' and 'subsidized a broad range of products' (Tuck and Lindert, 1996: viii). The reforms undertaken in Tunisia were different from those observed in most other countries and attempted to reduce the food subsidy by a combination of self-targeting and the introduction of quality differentiation. In other words, there was an attempt to demarcate 'inferior goods' from 'superior goods' and to provide a subsidy only on 'inferior goods'. It was assumed that because of the unattractive features of 'inferior goods', only the poor would consume them.

With the introduction of targeting in 1991, first, expenditure on food subsidies fell. In 1993, food subsidies accounted for 2 per cent of GDP and 6 per cent of government expenditure as compared to 4 per cent of GDP a decade earlier. Secondly, the share of food subsidies in total calorie and protein intake declined, with adverse effects on nutrition. A simulation exercise indicated that, on average, between 1990 and 1993, there was a 14 per cent fall in calorie intake and a 16 per cent fall in protein intake. The biggest impact came from the reduction in subsidies on bread wheat and durum wheat products. The impact was differential across income groups, with a 13.7 per cent loss in calorie intake among the poorest quintile. In

---

[6] The main source for this account is Tuck and Lindert (1996).

terms of protein intake, the reduction was higher among the lowest income quintile than the highest quintile.

The impact of food stamps

In recent times, advisers to the government of India and the World Bank have suggested a shift from rations to a system of food stamps or coupons (Bhagwati and Srinivasan 1993, World Bank 1996). What lessons can we learn from the experience of other countries including Mexico, Sri Lanka, Zambia and Jamaica that have introduced food stamps?[7]

One general lesson pertains to the administrative requirements of a food stamp programme as there are huge problems of administration both in respect of issuing of food stamps regularly and in respect of retail stores accepting stamps and being able to reimburse them easily. The administration of food stamps is a complex matter and many problems in implementation are possible. Detailed information is needed to identify and later revise the list of beneficiaries. A delivery mechanism for the regular issue of food stamps is required and extensive bookkeeping is required. Coupons may have to be re-validated from time to time; the possibility of exchanging them at different locations has to be worked out. The occurrence of fraud (such as by printing counterfeit coupons) has to be checked. For these reasons, the administration of food stamps in developing countries is not an easy matter.

The review of country experiences showed that if the objective of policy reform was to reduce spending, then targeted food stamps were a success in all countries. If, however, the criterion for judging policy reform is the extent of protection given to vulnerable individuals, then food stamps have failed miserably. In most countries (including Mexico, Sri Lanka and Jamaica), the reform of food subsidies as part of structural adjustment had adverse consequences for consumption and nutrition among the poor.

First, with the introduction of food stamp schemes, the real value of the subsidy was reduced. As stamps are denominated in nominal values, inflation erodes the real value of the subsidy to the consumer. In some situations, the increased purchasing power created by the scheme may

---

[7] See, also, von Braun et al. (1992) and Suryanarayana (1995b) for a review of food stamp programmes.

itself lead to a rise in prices.[8] In addition to general inflation, prices in stores that the poor purchase are often higher than prices in other stores. In all the schemes reviewed above, the real value of the subsidy was eroded when food stamps were introduced. At the same time, macro-economic changes such as devaluation led to a sharp rise in food prices. Secondly, the distribution of food stamps does not ensure physical availability of food or access to food. In Zambia, certain stores did not stock the commodities that could be purchased with food stamps, as they did not want to participate in the programme. Thirdly, many of the poorest were excluded from the scheme because of narrow targeting. Consequently, there was an increase in nutritional risk among some of the worst-off sections of the population, and consumption and nutrition outcomes deteriorated.

---

[8] See Suryanarayana (1995). Also, if sellers are monopolistic, they may raise prices when stamps are introduced (Rogers 1988).

six

Policy Changes
Since 1991

As noted in Chapter 4, PDS has many problems and limitations – the biggest one is its inadequacy in relation to the scale of the problem of hunger and vulnerability to hunger – and requires major overhaul. Instead of reforming the system so as to make it more effective, the specific solutions offered by the Central government in the post-1991 period of so-called 'structural adjustment' have led towards further dismantling and weakening of the delivery system. The first change has been in the principles underlying policy and objectives of PDS. The second feature of policy change has been the steady increase in food prices. Thirdly, there has been a decline in the supply of food to the distribution system. Fourthly, the policy has attempted to cut back coverage and consumption by means of targeting and a denial of the principle of universalism. Universal coverage, it is argued, is an extravagance that a poor country like India cannot afford. These policy changes are reflected in the specific schemes introduced during this period, the Revamped PDS (RPDS) in 1992 and Targeted PDS (TPDS) in 1997. Finally, although this is not the subject of this monograph, another major policy change of the 1990s has been the tendency to shift away from an agricultural strategy of self-sufficiency in food grain production.

This chapter explains how the policy changes of the 1990s have further dismantled PDS with serious implications for food security among the poorest of households.

Principles and objectives of policy

A cut back in subsidies, including a reduction in food subsidies, is one of the key tenets of programmes of orthodox structural adjustment throughout the world. Most subsidies are seen as wasteful by 'reformers' and reducing subsidies, including food subsidies, is seen as an important way of reducing public expenditure. In India too, the rhetoric of cutting down subsidies has been very strong in the period after 1991, and major changes in food policy have been motivated by the goal of expenditure reduction.

Since 1991, the central government has been looking at ways of reducing the food subsidy. The Government of India's *Economic Survey 1992–93* stated that 'while the public distribution system has to be continued to help the poor, the burden of subsidy on the central budget has also to be restrained' (GOI 1993: 92). The same document suggested that a 'phased withdrawal of food subsidies by targeting PDS' would help in the control of inflation (ibid.: 93). The following year, the government stated that 'whereas elimination of food subsidy is neither desirable nor feasible in the short and medium term, there is a strong reason to *contain* it' (GOI 1994a: 66, emphasis added). Advisers to the government have argued for reducing, even abolishing, food subsidies in order to reduce the fiscal deficit (e.g., Bhagwati and Srinivasan 1993).

Since even the promoters of orthodox structural adjustment now admit that these policies worsen deprivation, the suggested panacea is that reduction in food subsidies be accompanied by targeting. Two World Bank authors, for example, accept that economic shocks and adjustment polices 'raise the risk of deprivation among vulnerable groups' but then go on to argue that this only 'increases the urgency of targeting' (Pfefferman and Griffin 1989: 1). Thus, in the typical package of adjustment policies, the two major recommendations for consumer food subsidies are to reduce the total level of subsidy and to target the reduced subsidy to a limited group among the poorer section of the population. These shifts are evident in the policies of the Indian government.

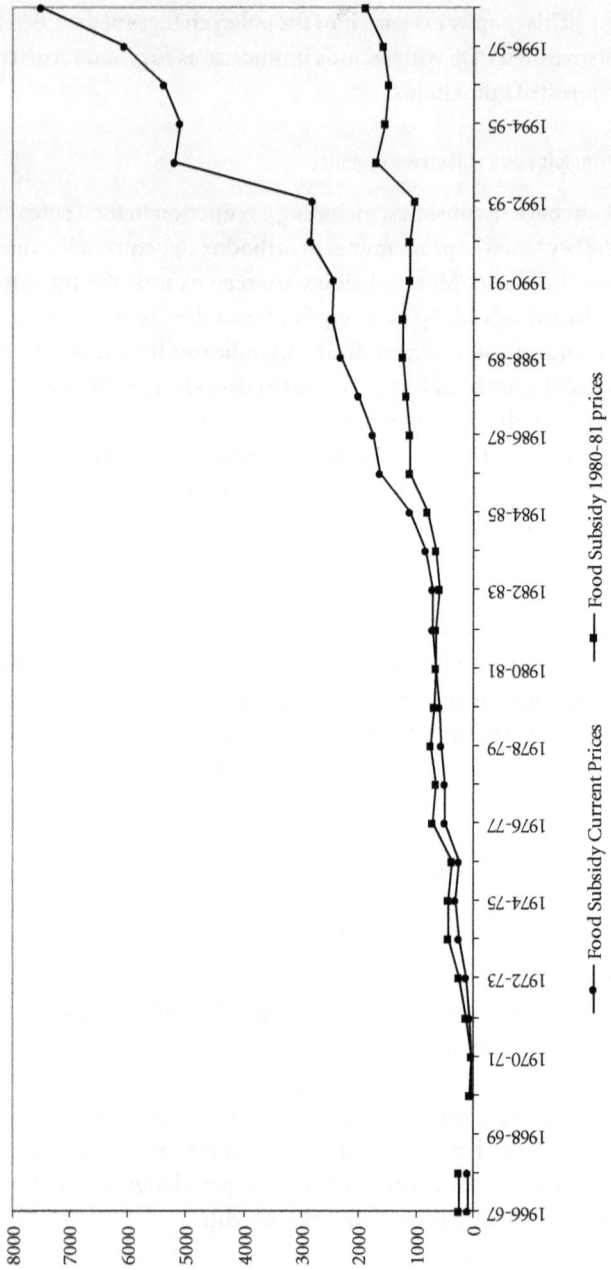

FIGURE 6.1 Expenditure on Food Subsidy, Current and 1980–81 prices, Rs. crores

Food subsidies in India: change in scale and scope

As the 'burden' of food subsidy has become central to the process of 'economic reforms', it is essential to examine the scale of food subsidies in India. How large is the food subsidy? How much has it grown over the last 30 years? The answer, as explained below, is that food subsidies have grown in nominal and real terms but if food subsidies are viewed in relation to GDP or government expenditures, the 'burden' has not changed much.

Graph 6.1 plots the central government's food subsidy at current prices and constant prices (deflated by the GDP deflator) over the years 1966–67 to 1997–98, and Graph 6.2 (overleaf) plots the nominal food subsidy as a proportion of GDP and as proportion of government expenditure over the same period. In nominal terms, the food subsidy has risen rapidly, particularly from the mid-1980s onwards with a big jump in 1993–94. At constant prices, the increase is subdued. Graph 6.1 shows that expenditure on food subsidy rose in the mid-1980s and then remained unchanged till about 1989–90. There was a dip between 1990–91 and 1992–93 followed by a rise in 1993–94. Food subsidies fell slightly in the following years but were higher than in the 1980s. However, when we look at food subsidy as a share of GDP then it has been more or less unchanged over the last 20 years, with a peak at about 0.64 per cent of GDP in 1993–94 and 0.63 in 1985–86. Interestingly, as a share of government expenditure, the food subsidy shows large year-to-year fluctuations.

What do these numbers indicate? First, in terms of a long-term trend, food subsidies as a share of GDP have not changed very much over the last twenty years. In other words, the 'burden' of food subsidy has not risen. Secondly, the food subsidy bill in India is not very high as compared to expenditures in other developing countries. In Sri Lanka, even after the introduction of means-tested food stamps, and a steep reduction in food subsidies, total food subsidies still accounted for 1.3 per cent of GDP (in 1984), or roughly twice the proportion in India (Jayawardena et al. 1988). In Mexico, in 1984, when general food subsidies had been eliminated, the food subsidy was 0.63 per cent of GDP (Pinstrup-Andersen et al. 1991). In Tunisia, food subsides were around 4 per cent of GDP in 1984 and they were reduced to around 2 per cent of GDP after targeting was introduced in 1993 (Tuck and Lindert 1996). In India, over the 31 year period, 1966–1997, food subsidy averaged 0.31 per cent of GDP and 2.35 per cent of

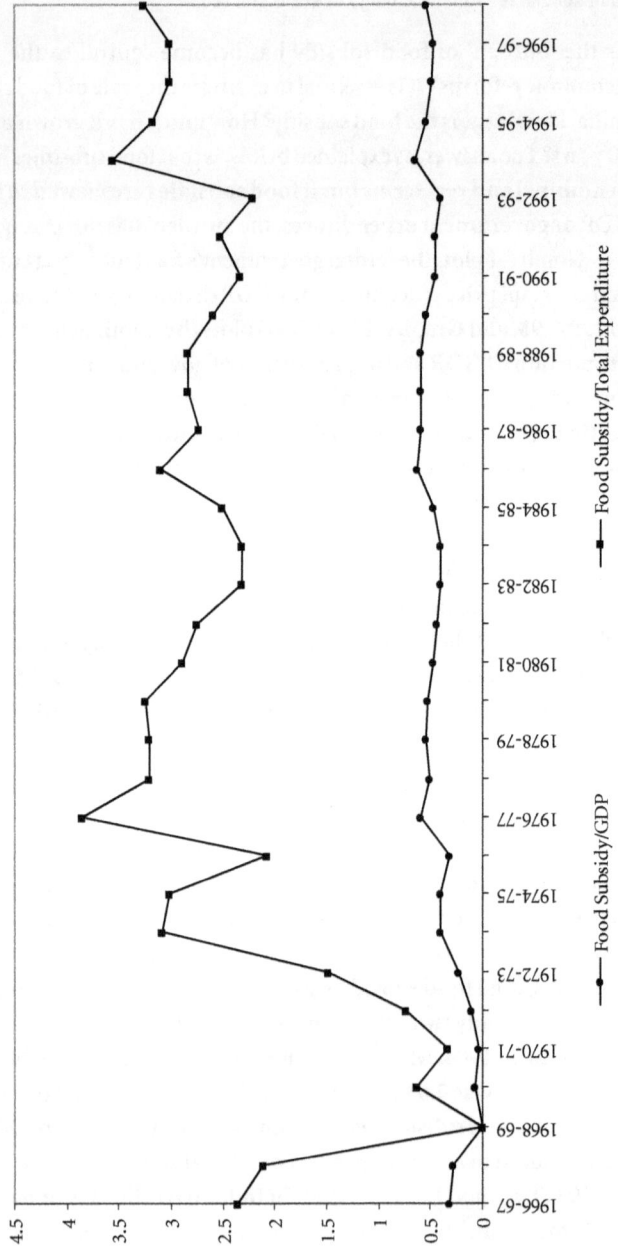

FIGURE 6.2 *Food subsidy as a proportion of GDP and total government expenditure*

Food Subsidy/Total Expenditure

Food Subsidy/GDP

central government expenditure. These numbers are important, to paraphrase Nora Lustig's comment on Mexico, because they show that even eliminating food subsidies totally will not solve the fiscal problems of the government (Lustig 1992).

Increase in food prices

In addition to a reduction in explicit food subsidies, structural adjustment usually entails a reduction in implicit food subsidies and the most obvious outcome of this is food price inflation. In India, one way of weakening the PDS in the early 1990s has been by means of a repeated rise over a very short period of time in the prices of commodities distributed in fair-price shops.

The changes in the central issue price of rice, of different types, and of wheat from 1980 onwards are plotted in Graphs 6.3 to 6.6 (pp. 84–87). These graphs show the dramatic increase that has taken place since the late 1980s (around 1989–90) in the prices of commodities supplied through the public distribution system. The central issue prices of commodities supplied to the PDS have been raised regularly in recent years. Between 1991 and 1994, the issue price of the common variety of rice rose 85.8 per cent and the issue price of wheat rose 71.8 per cent (Table 4.13). During the same period, the Index of Wholesale Prices rose 44.4 per cent. Between 1990–91 and 1994–95, the Consumer Price Index for Agricultural Labourers (CPIAL) rose 53.1 per cent. In other words, *the cumulative increase in the price of foodgrain sold through the PDS was higher than the corresponding increase in other general price indices.* The cumulative price increase was higher for rice of low quality, the common variety, than for rice of high quality, the superfine variety. The rise in issue prices was checked after 1994. Prices were held constant from 1994 to 1997 when a dual price regime was introduced as part of the Targeted PDS.

As prices of commodities in PDS increased at a faster rate than the market prices of similar commodities in many regions and for many commodities, the price differentials between the PDS and private markets narrowed or even disappeared. Price data from a market in Delhi, for example, showed that the difference between market and PDS prices for wheat fell from Rs 1.11 per kg. in January 1991 to 0.33 paisa per kg. in February 1994 (see GOI 1994a).

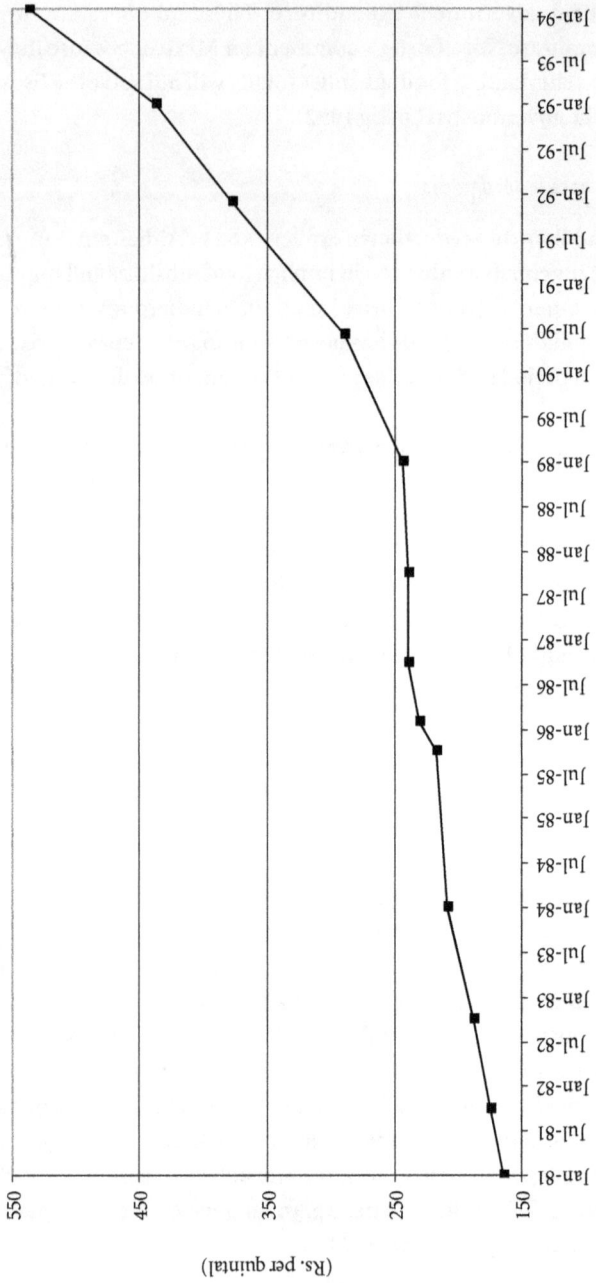

FIGURE 6.3 *Changes in central issue price of rice, common*

(Rs, per quintal)

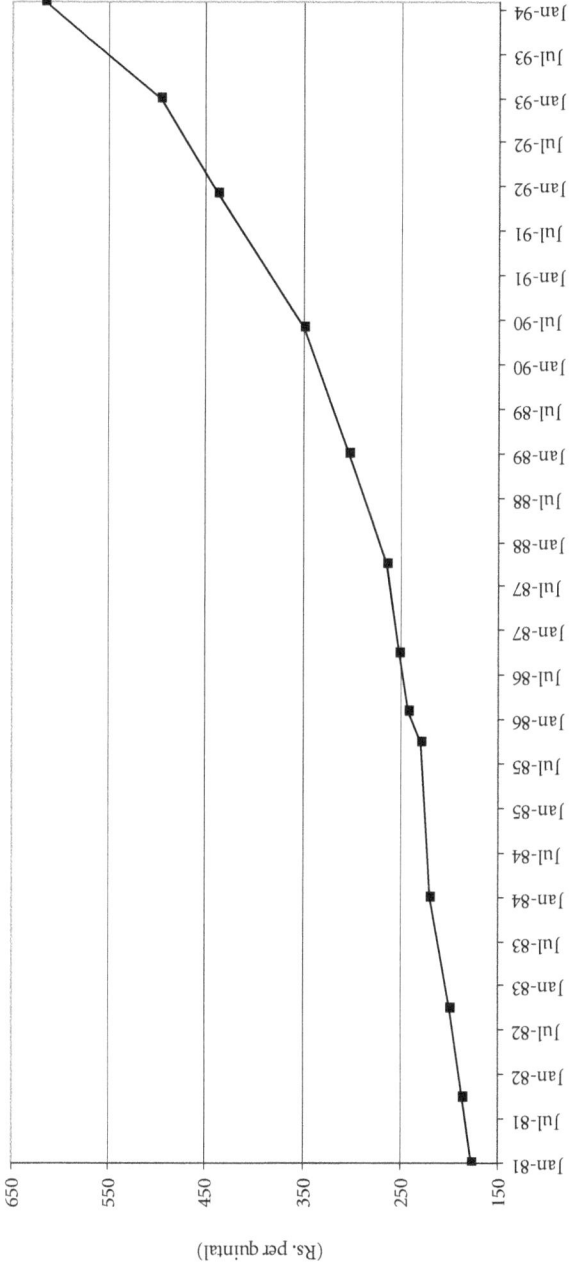

FIGURE 6.4 *Changes in central issue price of rice, fine*

FIGURE 6.5 *Changes in central issue price of rice, Superfine*

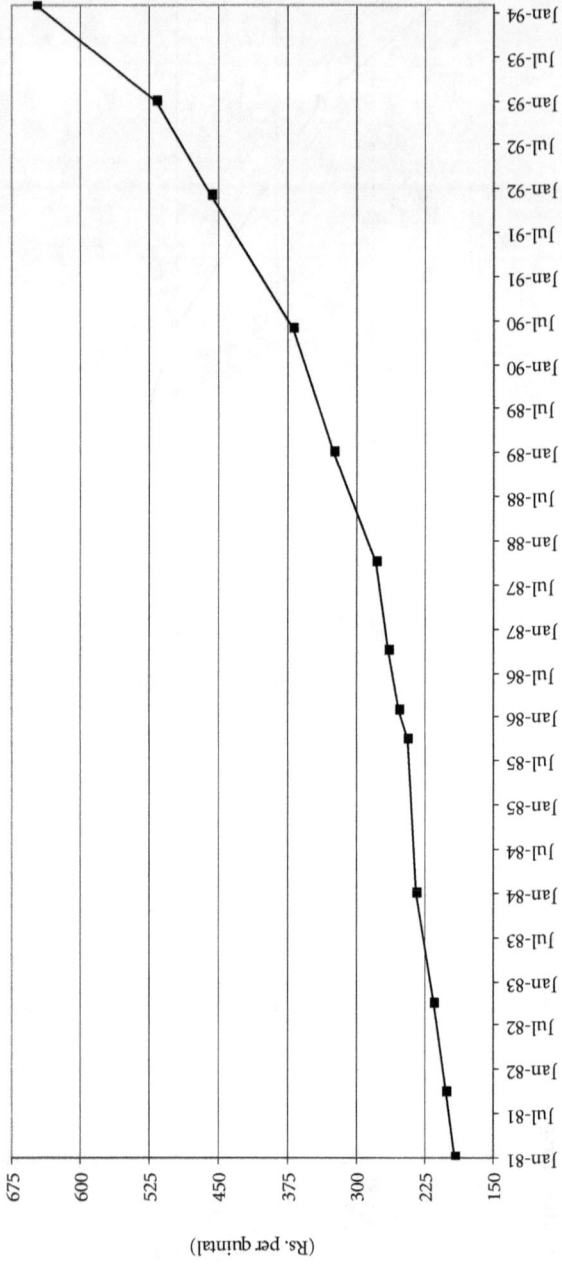

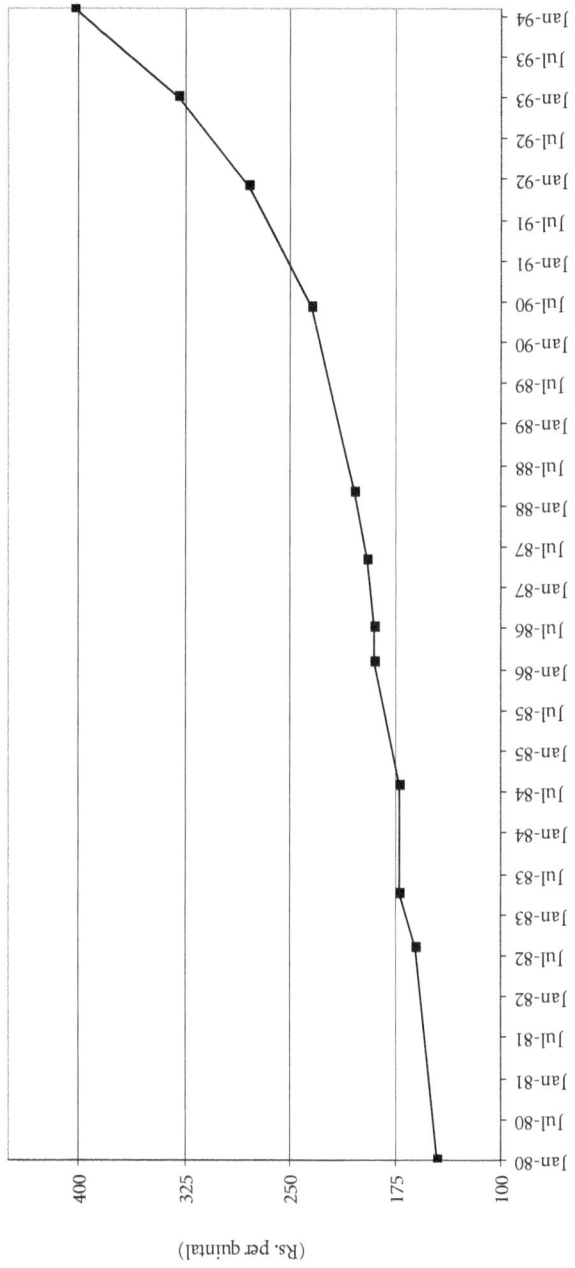

FIGURE 6.6 *Changes in central issue price of wheat*

In 1997, when TPDS started, prices of cereals for people below the poverty line ('BPL allocations') were kept low but prices for people above it ('APL allocations') rose substantially. The central issue prices for APL allocations were raised again in 1999, leading to sharp rises in state-level retail prices. The retail price of rice, for example, more than doubled between the end of 1997 and 1999 in three states (Himachal Pradesh, Jammu and Kashmir and Orissa). In the case of wheat also, retail prices for APL allocations were raised in most states in 1999. From 1994 to 1999, the central issue price for rice of grade A variety rose 43 per cent and the issue price of wheat rose 69.6 per cent.

In the economy as a whole, food prices were kept in check during the 1970s and 1980s and this was reflected in the fact that the real price of rice and wheat declined. As shown in Chapter 4, this trend was reversed in the 1990s. The real price of rice rose from 100 in 1981–82 to 111 in 1997–98, and the real price of wheat has also increased in the last few years. In short, in the 1990s, inflation in food prices has been high, and has raised the relative price of food (since food prices increased faster than general price indices such as the Index of Wholesale Prices).

Reduction in quantity distributed

Although the public distribution of food grain in India accounts for about 10 per cent of net availability, a striking feature of the data on quantities distributed is that *the supply of food grain to the public distribution system has declined sharply since 1991*. In 1991, 20.8 million tonnes of cereals were distributed in PDS (see Table 2.1). The quantity distributed fell steadily thereafter reaching 14 million tonnes in 1994. After 1994, the quantity distributed rose again but remained below 1992 levels. The decline was not on account of a fall in procurement. In fact there was a record procurement of 28 million tonnes in 1993 and of 26 million tonnes in 1994. While net availability of food grain declined slightly, the government maintained large buffer stocks. In fact, from July 1993 onwards, actual stocks were much higher than the norm in every quarter (Table 6.1). In January 1998, for example, 6.7 million tonnes of wheat were held as stocks. A year later, the stocks of wheat amounted to 12.7 million tonnes. Thus, in January 1999, taking rice and wheat together, the government held 7–8 million tonnes of food grain in excess of the stock norms.

In 1996, total offtake or distribution increased to around 18 million

TABLE 6.1 *Central pool stocks and minimum buffer stock norms for rice and wheat, 1990 to 1999 (in million tonnes)*

Beginning of the month	Wheat		Rice		Total food grain	
	Min. norm	Actual Stock	Min. norm	Actual Stock	Min. norm	Actual Stock
January – 1992	7.7	5.3	7.7	8.6	15.4	13.9
April	3.7	2.2	10.8	8.9	14.5	11.1
July	13.1	6.5	9.2	7.4	22.3	13.9
October	10.6	4.3	6.0	5.1	16.6	9.4
January – 1993	7.7	3.3	7.7	8.5	15.4	11.8
April	3.7	2.7	10.8	9.9	14.5	12.6
July	13.1	14.9	9.2	9.3	22.3	24.2
October	10.6	13.7	6.0	7.2	16.6	20.9
January – 1994	7.7	10.8	7.7	11.2	15.4	22.0
April	3.7	7.0	10.8	13.5	14.5	20.5
July	13.1	17.5	9.2	13.2	22.3	30.7
October	10.6	15.6	6.0	10.9	16.6	26.5
January – 1995	7.7	12.9	7.7	17.4	15.4	30.3
April	3.7	8.7	10.8	18.1	14.5	26.8
July	13.1	19.2	9.2	16.4	22.3	35.6
October	10.6	16.9	6.0	13.0	16.6	29.9
January – 1996	7.7	13.1	7.7	15.4	15.4	28.5
April	3.7	7.8	10.8	13.1	14.5	20.9
July	13.1	14.1	9.2	12.9	22.3	27.0
October	10.6	10.5	6.0	9.3	16.6	19.8
January – 1997	7.7	7.1	7.7	12.9	15.4	20.0
April	3.7	3.2	10.8	13.2	14.5	16.4
July	13.1	11.4	9.2	11.0	22.3	22.4
October	10.6	8.3	6.0	7.0	16.6	15.3
January – 1998	7.7	6.7	7.7	11.5	15.4	18.2
April	3.7	5.1	10.8	13.0	14.5	18.1
July	13.1	16.5	9.2	12.0	22.3	28.5
October	10.6	15.2	6.0	9.0	16.6	24.2
January – 1999	8.4	12.7	8.4	11.7	16.8	24.4

Notes Min. norm stands for the minimum norm for buffer stock holdings.
There are new norms for buffer stocks from October 30, 1998.
Total food grain, here, refers to rice and wheat together.
Source *Economic Survey,* different years.

tonnes. Offtake declined in 1997 and rose again in 1998. Provisional data for 1998–99 indicate a small rise in offtake as compared to 1997–98 but the level remained below that of 1996. The total offtake remains below the peak of 20.8 million tonnes reached in 1991. Moreover, recent evidence indicates that offtake of wheat from PDS in the first few months of the 1999 fiscal year (April–September) is lower than the offtake in the corresponding period for 1998 (Damodaran 1999).

In the aftermath of the introduction of structural adjustment policy, per capita offtake has also declined. Between 1991 and 1995, per capita offtake of food grain from PDS declined in most states (see Table 4.4). Although there was an increase in offtake in several states between 1995 and 1998, the major feature of the period 1991 to 1998, in a large number of states, was a fall in the per capita offtake of food grain.

Thus, paradoxically, the early years of structural adjustment were characterized by a rise in stocks of food grain on the one hand, and a fall in offtake of food grain, on the other (see Patnaik 1997).

Introduction of targeting: Revamped PDS and Targeted PDS

As part of the programme of structural adjustment, specific changes were made to the PDS in the 1990s to incorporate new principles of targeting. The Revamped PDS involved targeting specific areas, with special preference given to 'the population living in the most difficult areas of the country, such as drought-prone areas, desert areas, tribal areas, certain designated hilly areas and urban slum areas' (GOI 1992). In 1997, the government of India introduced Targeted PDS in an attempt to target households on the basis of an income criterion, that is, use the income poverty line to demarcate 'poor' and 'non-poor' households. The objective was 'to streamline the PDS by issuing special cards to families below the poverty line and selling essential articles under the PDS to them at specially subsidized prices, with better monitoring of the delivery system' (GOI 1997: 1). There has been no large-scale national evaluation by means of detailed surveys of the impact of these two new policies. The impact of the Revamped PDS (or RPDS) is assessed here by means of field studies of a RPDS village in Maharashtra. The impact of TPDS has yet to be studied empirically. However, some of the problems of targeting, in principle and in practice, can be identified.

Revamped PDS

In 1992, the Government of India introduced a new scheme, termed the Revamped PDS, that was targeted at selected backward areas of the country. The objectives of RPDS were:

1. to increase coverage of the population in the target areas;
2. to improve the access of income-poor consumers to the public distribution system;
3. to increase the range of commodities supplied by fair-price shops; and
4. to provide selected commodities at prices lower than in the general PDS.

To implement the Revamped PDS, the Government of Maharashtra introduced a Special Action Plan for 115 *tehsils*, of which 68 *tehsils* were defined as 'tribal areas'. The Plan included provisions for setting up new fair-price shops, for introducing mobile shops, and for supplying additional commodities such as tur dal (pigeon pea), tea powder, iodized salt, washing and bathing soap to ration-card holders. Lastly, special prices and quantities were announced for the Revamped PDS areas.

In 1995–96, I conducted a census type village survey of a RPDS village in Maharashtra – Akhar village in Jawhar *taluka* of Thane district. Akhar village is populated wholly by persons of the scheduled tribes. The village is remote, located off the road from Jawhar to Jhap, with only a couple of bus services on this route every day. The village is characterized by dryland agriculture: cultivation occurs only during the monsoon, as there is no source of irrigation.

Entitlements in PDS

Entitlements differ as between the Revamped PDS and non-Revamped PDS areas. As indicated in Table 6.2 (overleaf), paradoxically, food grain entitlements are lower in the revamped PDS area than in areas under the general PDS. Thus, for families in Revamped PDS areas, *the entitlements of food grain have been reduced*. Before 1992, each adult was entitled to buy 10 kg. of grain a month at a subsidized rate from fair-price shops; the entitlements of a household were based on the number of members of a household. In the new scheme, a uniform ceiling of 20 kg. of grain per

TABLE 6.2: *Ration scale in general and Revamped PDS, Maharashtra (kg. per month)*

Commodity	General PDS	Revamped PDS
Rice	4 kg. for 2 units*	20 kg. a card#
Wheat	6 kg. for 2 units*	
Sugar	425 grams per capita	425 grams per capita
Cooking oil	1 kg. per card	1 kg. per card
Dal	2 kg. per card	2 kg. per card
Salt	Nil	1 kg. per card
Tea	Nil	250 grams per card
Washing/Bathing soap	Nil	2 cakes per card

Notes   Adult = 2 units; child = 1 unit.
   *   here is a ceiling of 30 kg. of grain per card.
   #   This includes rice and wheat together.
Source   *Economic Survey of Maharashtra 1994–95*, Table 13.1.

month per household was introduced. Entitlements of food grain were thus reduced for all households with more than two adults in RPDS. Further, for households in areas regulated by the old PDS scheme, a ceiling of 30 kg. per family per month was announced the same year. The scale for sugar, oil and pulses were, however, the same in the two areas. In RPDS areas, additional commodities supplied were salt, tea and soap.

Price changes

In Maharashtra, a state where retail prices in fair-price shops are among the highest in the country, prices of ration rice and wheat rose even faster than at the national level. Between 1991 and 1994, the issue price of the common variety of rice rose 94.1 per cent and the price of wheat rose 85 per cent. Further, as at the national level, the price increase for cereals supplied through PDS was higher than the cumulative increase in consumer price indices. Between 1990–91 and 1994–95 in Maharashtra, the Rural Consumer Price Index rose 47.7 per cent and CPIAL 56.5 per cent.

The sharp increase in issue prices in PDS has lowered price differentials between PDS and open market prices. In Akhar village, price differences between the private store and the ration shop were very small and less than a rupee for the common variety of rice (Rs 0.30 to 0.70). For the superfine variety, the price difference was around Rs 1 to Rs 1.50. Price differences were, however, large for wheat flour, sugar, salt and oil.

Table 6.3 *Offtake of rice and wheat in the general and revamped PDS, Maharashtra, 1991–95 (in lakh tonnes)*

Year	All PDS areas			Revamped PDS areas		
	Rice	Wheat	Total	Rice	Wheat	Total
1991	6.62	12.78	19.4	n.a.	n.a.	n.a.
1992	7.5	11.57	19.07	n.a.	n.a.	n.a.
1993	6.34	5.48	11.82	1.28	1.69	2.97
1994	3.83	4.9	8.73	1.19	1.67	2.86
1995	3.61	6.39	10.0	1.68	2.62	4.3
1996	5.82	9.27	15.09	1.71	2.65	4.36
1997*	5.79	9.04	14.83	0.70	0.81	1.51
1998	6.3	11.31	17.61			

Note The data refers to quantity of food grain issued to fair-price shops in the state.
   * Data on RPDS are for January–May 1997.
Source *Economic Survey of Maharashtra*, different years.

Coverage, utilization and quantity distributed

With lower entitlements and higher prices, it is not surprising that the quantities of commodities sold by fair-price shops have fallen since 1991. The data show that supply of both wheat and rice fell sharply between 1992 and 1995 in PDS. The sale of wheat and rice from fair price shops in 1995 was around half of that in 1992 (Table 6.3). In RPDS regions, offtake of rice and wheat fell initially, between 1992 and 1993, and then rose from 1993 to 1994.

Observations from the village study illustrate some specific failures of RPDS.

• In Akhar village, 20 (or 17 per cent) of the 116 households in the survey did not possess a ration card. Clearly, full coverage of households was not achieved in RPDS.
• In Akhar village, nearly 88 per cent of households purchased neither rice nor wheat from the ration shop during the reference month (90 per cent purchased no rice and 92 per cent purchased no wheat). Secondly, no household purchased dal, tea, salt or soap from the ration shop in May 1996. Only one household purchased palmolein oil. Sugar was also not purchased by the large majority (91 per cent) of households.

In short, the coverage of RPDS was not universal and utilization was low. The purchase of food grain from PDS was not a regular monthly feature for most households, and the contribution of PDS to monthly cereal consumption was small. Clearly, RPDS did not improve the access of the poor to PDS.

Targeted PDS

The essence of TPDS is delineated, as follows, in a Government of India document called *Focus on the Poor* (GOI 1997).

> To start with, it is proposed to issue 10 kg. of food grain per family per month, at specially subsidized prices for all families below the poverty line as per the estimates for 1993–94 arrived at by the Planning Commission using the methodology of the Expert Group under Prof. Lakdawala. Further, as recommended by the Conference of Chief Ministers, the average lifting of food grain for the last 10 years by the States is proposed to be continued for the benefit of the population above the poverty line at present getting the benefit of PDS. The quantity of food grain out of this average lifting (offtake) which is in excess of the requirement for the population below poverty line, is proposed to be allocated to States as a transitory allocation, at the central issue prices (ibid.).

The document also has guidelines on the identification of the population below the poverty line, provision of special cards, scale of supply, issue price of commodities and certain aspects of review, transparency and monitoring.

Targeted PDS differs from all earlier programmes in certain major respects. First, a distinction between 'below-poverty-line' (BPL) and 'above-poverty-line' (APL) populations is introduced with the two groups treated differently in terms of quantities and prices.[1] With this, the Government of India has initiated a policy of narrow targeting of PDS on households with incomes below the official poverty line. Secondly, the principle of entitlements has been altered from a per capita norm to a

---

[1] Although some state governments had systems of dual or multiple ration cards prior to 1997, this is the first time the distinction has been made by the central government.

family norm. Ration scales are typically defined in terms of certain quantities per person or per unit (with an adult equivalent to two units, and a child equivalent to one unit). In Targeted PDS, however, each poor family, irrespective of size and need, is entitled to a uniform quantity of food grain. Thirdly, the monthly entitlement for the 'poor' has been fixed at the meagre level of 10 kg. In other words, Targeted PDS ensures poor households the pitiful quantity of about 2 to 3 kg. per person per month! State governments are advised to revise and lower their ration scales to match the new principle of allocation. For example, with reference to states that offer 15 kg. per person (the norm recommended by ICMR), the guidelines note that 'it will not be possible to maintain such an *inflated* scale of issue (ibid.: 3, emphasis added). Additional allocations demanded by states from the central pool are to be provided at commercially viable prices. So state governments can (and some do) provide more than 10 kg. of grain to each poor family but they will have to bear the higher costs. Lastly, for 'non-poor' households, a transitory allocation is envisaged, one that is based on past levels of utilization (although the period of transition is unspecified). To put it differently, there is no longer a guaranteed entitlement for households classified as being 'above the poverty line'. The principle of universal coverage is clearly being abandoned. There is also a flaw in the reasoning used to arrive at the magical number of ten kilos per family. This number was derived on the assumption that if currently available food grain (16 to 17 million tonnes) were distributed to 165 million households (the entire population), then each household would get around 100 kg. a year. However, TPDS offers 10 kg. to poor households only and does not guarantee any fixed quantity of food grain for households above the poverty line. By a disingenuous argument, the undernourished have been short-changed.

Pitfalls of targeting
Given fixed resources, targeting appears to have the advantage of giving more to selected sections of the population, say the 'poor'. The choice between targeted and universal schemes, however, as we demonstrate in Appendix 6A, is not a simple one. There are many costs of targeting, and these costs can be large. The theoretical problems associated with targeting are discussed in the Appendix. Here I give some examples of the practical problems of targeting.

The official poverty line, a useful academic tool for understanding and monitoring poverty, cannot be easily used to demarcate one set of households from another on the ground. Specifically, the identification of the poor, for purposes of targeting, on the basis of an income criterion has many problems. First, the accuracy of data on incomes in household surveys, such as the baseline survey conducted for the Integrated Rural Development Programme (IRDP), is dubious. In a country where the majority of the population works in the informal sector and receives earnings on an irregular basis, income is very difficult to measure. Secondly, for households that earn income from casual labour or from self-employment, incomes fluctuate over time, and even from day to day, a classification based on incomes reported on the day of a survey may be a very inaccurate basis for calculating incomes over the year. Thirdly, given that the official poverty line in India is very low (Chapter 3), a household that earns ten or fifty or even a hundred rupees more than the poverty-line level of income is not necessarily less vulnerable than a household with income below the poverty line. To sum up, there is large scope for misidentifying households and for mis-targeting when an income-poverty line is used.

Take the case of Maharashtra (see Moghe 1997). When Targeted PDS was announced, according to the central government, 36.8 per cent of households or about 60 lakh households were eligible for the BPL category, based on the Expert Group's estimation of poverty (GOI 1997). To the state government fell the task of matching this number of officially poor families with specific ration cardholders. To identify eligible households, the state government turned to the baseline surveys conducted for the implementation of IRDP. For purposes of IRDP, a poor household was defined as one with an annual income of less than Rs 11,000. The IRDP surveys conducted in 1992–93 showed that the state had 77.6 lakh poor households in rural areas. As this number was higher than the figure given by the Expert Group, the state decided to restrict eligibility to the 'poorest' within the IRDP surveys, namely households with less than Rs 4,000 a year, and so reduced the number of eligible households to 43 lakh. In short, to implement Targeted PDS, the state decided to exclude households that had been identified officially as 'poor' for the IRDP scheme. About 34 lakh families were thus redefined as 'not poor' for the purposes of PDS. In urban areas, as there was no equivalent household income survey, the process of identifying BPL families was utterly arbitrary.[2] In slum settlements, for example, households were classified as BPL or APL on the basis of a few queries, such as the occupation of the main earner of the family. This has resulted in absurdly low numbers of BPL families. In Dharavi, the slum settlement in Bombay with a population of half a million, the Rationing Control Officer identified only 365 families as belonging to the BPL category in 1997, and after 're-checks', the number fell to 151 in 1999. The whole process of identification has resulted in large errors of misclassification with genuinely deserving households excluded and some affluent households included in the BPL category (Moghe 1997).

Implications of changes in prices and quantities

After the introduction of TPDS, central issue prices for allocations to BPL families were lower than earlier prices for RPDS and PDS allocations. For BPL allocations, the central issue price announced was Rs 3.50 a kilo for the common variety of rice and Rs 3 for wheat. At the same time, central issue prices were raised substantially for allocations under the APL category. For example, before TPDS, central issue prices for rice ranged from Rs 5.37 to Rs 6.48, and after the implementation of TPDS, central issue prices for APL allocations were between Rs 5.50–7.00. As a consequence, in most states, the prices of wheat and rice for households above the poverty line rose steeply after the introduction of TPDS. In Rajasthan, for example, the price of grade A rice (fine and superfine varieties) rose from Rs 6.70–7.00 before TPDS to Rs 9.70 after TPDS, an increase of around 40 percent. There were, however, some exceptions (such as Kerala). Note that states can purchase additional quantities of grains at APL prices and distribute them to all households including BPL families.

As noted in Chapter 4, the distribution of total offtake across states has changed after TPDS was implemented. The states that earlier topped the ranking by share of all-India offtake lost their position between 1995 and 1998. Kerala maintained its share but the share of Andhra Pradhesh, Tamil Nadu, West Bengal and Karnataka fell. These changes stem from the new principles of allocation, namely the guaranteeing of 10 kg. only to the officially recognized BPL population and quantity restrictions for the 'non-poor'. States that were providing more than 10 kg. of food grain

---

[2] Officials of the Department of Food and Civil Supplies admitted this (pers. comm.).

have to now buy the additional quantity at higher prices even for distribution to the BPL population. The new policy thus constitutes an 'attack on the PDS in those states where it has been functioning well' (Chandrasekhar and Ghosh, 1997).

Further, there are major differences between states in the division of total offtake as between BPL and APL categories, depending on the initial strength of PDS in the state. This can be illustrated with data on offtake for the period January to December 1998. In Bihar, a state where the functioning of PDS is known to be weak, offtake has risen sharply after TPDS came about, and offtake of rice and wheat in the BPL category was about five times higher than offtake in the APL category. Given a weak distribution system and relatively low offtake in the past, the state appears now to be only purchasing the cheaper grain allocated for distribution to BPL households. It is difficult to say whether this grain actually reached BPL households or whether it was profitably siphoned off to other consumers. In Kerala, by contrast, offtake under the APL category was 16 times greater than the BPL offtake in the state. This reflects both the fact that the state was allocated higher quantities of APL grain on the basis of past allocations, and that the state was committed to supplying a certain quantity of food grain to the entire population served by PDS. The government of Kerala offered a higher quantity to BPL households than the allocation from the centre, as well as providing for the APL population. As there is a large price difference between BPL and APL allocations, (and additional allocations are even more expensive), it is clear that state governments that are committed to providing a certain minimum quantity of food grain to their population have to now bear the burden of higher costs.

Given changes in prices and in entitlements, how did the typical poor family fare? Take the situation in Maharashtra. In RPDS, a tribal family could have purchased up to 20 kg. of rice of common variety at Rs 4.40 per kilo, thus spending Rs 88 in total. In TPDS, if classified as BPL, the family could buy its entire quota of 10 kg. at Rs 4.00. If the remaining 10 kg. were purchased from PDS, assuming it was available, at the special rate of Rs 5.20 (for tribal areas), the family would have to spend Rs 92 for 20 kg. of rice. If the family were to buy the additional 10 kilos in the market, the expenditure would be even higher. If a family in a backward area were classified as APL, as is likely to be the case for the large majority of households in RPDS areas, the amount a family needs to spend on the same quantity of grain would be even higher.

In other words, although prices for BPL allocations are low and have remained constant since 1997, the sharp rise in APL prices combined with the lower entitlements for BPL families means that the expenditure on basic food grain would have risen even for families correctly identified as poor families. For the large number of genuinely deserving families that have the misfortune to be classified as 'above the poverty line' under the new dispensation, the minimum cost of purchasing grain from PDS would have risen significantly.

Final remarks

This chapter has argued that there has been a major shift in the policy objectives of the Government of India after the introduction of structural adjustment in 1991. In line with programmes of structural adjustment, the twin goals of policy are to reduce food subsidies and introduce targeting. The 'burden' of food subsidy, it should be pointed out, has not risen over time, as the ratio of food subsidies to GDP has remained at about half a per cent of GDP over the last twenty years. Nevertheless, there is no longer a commitment to universal coverage. After 1991, PDS was weakened by means of repeated increases in the prices of commodities supplied and by means of a reduction in the quantities supplied. Issue prices of grain in PDS have risen steadily since the late 1980s. The prices of rice and wheat supplied in fair-price shops rose steeply between 1992 and 1994, and the rate of increase exceeded the general rate of inflation. Further, the long-term trend decline in the real price of rice and wheat appears to have been reversed in recent years. The offtake from PDS also declined sharply in the immediate post-1991 period. Two new schemes of targeting were introduced in the 1990s. The first scheme, Revamped PDS, attempted geographical or area targeting in order to expand coverage in selected backward areas of the country. A case study of a RPDS village in Maharashtra showed that coverage was not universal and utilization remained low even after 'revamping'. The second scheme, Targeted PDS, was introduced in a situation in which quantities distributed in PDS were declining, and where many poor households were already excluded from PDS. TPDS initiated targeting on the basis of the income-poverty line, with a guarantee of provision only for households below the official poverty line. We illustrated the enormous practical problems in targeting on the basis of income and argued that administrative targeting, based on a narrow income cut-off, will lead to the further exclusion of vulnerable households from the system. The costs of targeting are elaborated on in the Appendix that follows. There have been certain other major changes in policy as part of TPDS. Entitlements have been reduced. The quantity of food grain that is guaranteed for a 'poor' household is now only 10 kg., a measly proportion of the quantity of grain needed for subsistence. This quantity is fixed for all households, irrespective of household size. Given the changes in prices and entitlements, I argued that poor households would have to spend more to purchase their basic minimum requirements of grain. Further, the new principle of allocation has penalized states that were distributing larger quantities of food grain relative to others prior to targeting. To sum up, given the serious conceptual and practical problems in the design of TPDS, it is doomed to fail in improving the access of the poor to PDS.

appendix 6A

The Costs of Targeting

The choice between targeted and universal transfers depends on a host of factors that determine the relative costs and benefits of each type of transfer. In this Appendix, I outline the factors that need to be examined prior to making a choice between targeted and universal schemes (see, e.g., Burgess and Stern 1991, and Sen 1992, 1995).

Rights or entitlements

The fundamental argument for universal transfers is that based on rights. All human beings have a right to a decent life, and therefore, to minimum food, basic education, health and other goods or services that provide for a decent life. The Indian government was one of the signatories to the Rome Declaration on World Food Security, affirming 'the fundamental right of everyone to be free from hunger'.

Targeting errors or errors of inclusion and exclusion

Typically, there are two types of errors that occur in any targeted welfare programme due to problems of measurement.[1] Errors of wrong exclusion

---

[1]   There is a useful discussion of these issues in Cornia and Stewart (1993).

(called Type I errors) refer to the exclusion of genuinely poor or deserving households from a programme. The second type of errors, namely errors of wrong inclusion, (called Type II errors) refer to the inclusion of non-eligible persons or households in a programme. Universal programmes tend to have large errors of wrong inclusion (that is, include the rich) but small errors of wrong exclusion. On the other hand, narrowly targeted programmes tend to have small errors of wrong inclusion but large errors of wrong exclusion. The more fine the targeting, the more the likelihood of Type I errors, that is, of wrongly excluding the needy. Practical experience with universal and targeted food subsidy programmes in developing countries has shown that universal or general subsidies were associated with large errors of inclusion. When targeted programmes were introduced, while errors of inclusion fell, there was a big increase in the errors of exclusion (see Chapter 5).

When one type of errors increases, the other type of error decreases. We thus need to trade-off between these types of errors. What weights to do we attach to the two types of errors? Are they equally important? If we attach a high weight to errors of wrong exclusion, that is, we try to minimize the number of households that are wrongly excluded, then a universal scheme will be preferred to a targeted scheme. *However, if a high weight is attached to errors of wrong inclusion then targeted schemes will be preferred.* Any decision therefore calls for some judgement about the relative importance of the two types of errors. In making such a judgement, we should note that there is a basic asymmetry in the costs attached to the two types of errors. Errors of wrong inclusion result in fiscal or financial cost, that is, higher expenditure due to the inclusion of wrong or ineligible beneficiaries. Errors of wrong exclusion, however, lead to welfare costs, that is, the costs to individuals and society due to inadequacy of food, malnutrition, etc. While fiscal costs are known and easy to measure, it is more difficult to measure the welfare costs of undernutrition.

One attempt to value the welfare cost of undernutrition in monetary terms was made by Giovanni Cornia and Frances Stewart (1993). They examined the effects of undernutrition on (a) short-term labour productivity, (b) long term productivity via phenomena such as growth retardation, and (c) inter-generational variables such as reproductive efficiency. To take a concrete example, they looked at the impact of malnutrition among mothers on the birth weight, health and potential of the next generation.

To assess the welfare loss associated with malnutrition, they attempted to measure the future income foregone as a consequence of lower productivity stemming from malnutrition. Their results indicated that the welfare costs of excluding the poor from programmes of food subsidy were large.

The costs of administration

The costs of administration of a welfare programme depend on the nature of existing institutions and delivery mechanisms, and on the extent of information available. Targeting raises the costs of delivery and administration, as the target group has to be identified on the basis of specified criteria. Targeting involves greater administrative capabilities and expenses. If information on personal incomes is perfect and can be obtained at little cost, then, of course, it becomes easier to segregate and target individuals by some criterion like income. In developing countries, given both the structure of the economy (e.g., a large agricultural and self-employed sector) and the ability of administrative organizations to collect accurate information, perfect information and perfect targeting are impossible to achieve. It is in this context that targeting is likely to raise the costs of administration. Costs are, however, likely to vary with the type of targeting. Targeting by a criterion such as geographical residence may be easier to implement and less costly than targeting by income or nutritional status. In developing countries, administrative costs have risen with a shift from universal to targeted welfare programmes (Cornia and Stewart 1993).[2] The administration of a targeted programme is undoubtedly more complex than that of a universal transfer and requires greater administrative competence and costs more.

Incentive and information distortions

To qualify for a targeted programme, participants may distort information or their incentives may be altered. Targeting can, for instance, create an incentive to cheat. In particular, when targeting is by means of administrative methods such as means testing then the scope for misuse rises. In this respect, narrow targeting is likely to be worse than broad targeting for the

---

[2] In developed countries too, the costs of administering targeted programmes are generally higher than that of universal transfers (Besley and Kanbur, 1993).

following reasons. When the number of eligible persons is reduced, there are, of course, a larger number of non-eligible persons who may try to cheat. Similarly, when resources are restricted, more cheating may occur to gain access to the limited resources available. To prevent misuse, it may be better to define the target group more broadly.

Social stigma and cohesion.

Targeting has social costs that arise from the stigma attached to recipients of targeted welfare programmes. Targeting can be invasive and intrusive and result in greater social divisions. Segregating households on the basis of incomes in a country where the poverty line reflects a very low absolute level of income, and where there is a fluidity of households around the poverty line, can lead to social tensions and polarization.

Loss of quality

When programmes that are universal become targeted, the quality tends to deteriorate as the oft-heard phrase 'programmes for the poor are poor programmes' suggests (see van de Walle 1995). Targeted programmes often end up being inferior to universal programmes.

Costs of participation

Initial costs are usually higher for participation in a targeted programme than in a universal programme. Participation may be limited by the costs of take-up. A key factor in take-up is information about the programme and about the conditions for eligibility.

Political support and long run costs

Targeting may reduce political support for a programme, and reduced support can result in lower allocations for a targeted programme. To put it differently, assuming a fixed budget, perfect targeting at no or low costs could give higher benefits to the poor or the target group. However, the budget allocation may itself change depending on the type of programme, and typically, allocations fall when a programme becomes targeted. So, if the budget support for a programme is made endogenous, then targeting may be worse for the poor than a system of universal transfers. There is a good body of evidence, from developed and less developed countries, that political support differs as between universal and targeted transfers. The differences in political support get reflected in the size of transfers, both in per capita terms and in terms of total transfers, and in the very continuation or dismantling of a programme. In Sri Lanka, for example, a switch from a universal to a targeted food subsidy resulted, over time, in a steep reduction in benefits (Chapter 5). In Colombia, a food subsidy programme was targeted out of existence (Pinstrup-Andersen 1993).

In their book, *Not Only the Poor: The Middle Classes and the Welfare State*, Goodin and Le Grand (1987) make a case for why it may be beneficial to include the non-poor, particularly the middle classes, in social security and other welfare programmes. They argue that the 'non-poor play a crucial role in creating, expanding, sustaining, reforming and dismantling the welfare state' (ibid.). Thus, the inclusion of the middle classes in a welfare programme can be on 'purely pragmatic' grounds for they are likely to vote and support the continuation of programmes they benefit from, and very importantly, defend them at the time of expenditure cuts.

Choice of the degree of targeting

The listing of factors above has shown that the choice between targeted and universal transfers is a complex one, and depends on the weights attached to different costs. There are some strong arguments for universal transfers, from the perspective of theory and the experience of countries. One argument for universal coverage comes from the perspective of rights. Another strong argument for universal transfers derives from issues of political support. Social concerns like cohesion, and concerns for participation can also be used to support universal transfers. However, the most important factor, particularly in poor and less developed countries, is the costs of exclusion. If the goal of policy is to ensure food security to all vulnerable persons, it leads right away to an emphasis on lowering the errors of wrong exclusion, and hence to a preference for universal programmes.

In the short run, there may be a trade-off between fiscal objectives and welfare objectives, as targeting narrowly can lower fiscal costs. In the long or medium-run, however, when all costs are measured and valued, universal transfers may be more cost-effective. Although the literature on comparisons of alternative welfare programmes is limited, the conclusion of most studies is that the benefits of targeting over universal transfers are quite limited, if any (Lipton and Ravallion, 1995).

A point that is often missed is that a universal programme need not provide uniform benefits to all participants. A universal service, for instance, can be financed by selective taxes and when the total effect of taxes and transfers is examined the provision of the service is no longer uniform for all participants. In fact, when the costs of targeting are high, there is a good case for universal provision accompanied by tax claw-backs from the rich. Or, when the target group is large, it makes sense to provide benefits universally and then to claw-back benefits from the rich.

seven

What Needs to be Done

A Strategy to Reform PDS

This chapter considers specific proposals needed to strengthen PDS and make it an effective means of providing food security. I begin, first, with the officially endorsed 'consensus' view of targeting and try to establish why we need a system of broad targeting or near-universal coverage in India and not a system of narrow poverty-line-level-of-income-based targeting. Secondly, I discuss the need for more food in the system in order to ensure minimum nutritional support. Thirdly, there is the critical issue of keeping food prices in control. Fourthly, the system of production and procurement has to be strengthened and modified to meet the requirements of an expanded PDS. Fifthly, it is essential to improve the administration of the entire system and the functioning of fair-price shops. Lastly, programmes of employment generation and other means of creating purchasing power among the mass of population have to be combined with subsidized food distribution programmes such as PDS to ensure that the poorest have access to adequate food.

Universal coverage or the case against narrow targeting

In the context of fiscal crises and structural adjustment, a frequent response of governments, as shown in Chapter 5, has been to cut food subsidies by means of targeting the benefits to a narrow section of the population. The Indian government too has attempted different forms of targeting in the 1990s, and since 1997, initiated a scheme of targeting on the basis of the official poverty line. Orthodox reformers are not satisfied and there are studies that advocate even narrower targeting. A report by the World Bank has, for instance, recommended that PDS be targeted to the very poor, that is, 'distinguish between the very poor and the moderately poor and improve efficacy of PDS in transferring food to the ultra-poor' (World Bank 1996: 16). The 'very poor' are defined as those households that have expenditures less than three-fourths of the official poverty line level of expenditure. The moderately poor are the remaining households with expenditures below the poverty line. In short, an extremely narrow form of targeting is being propagated: not just targeting to those below the official poverty line, a very low absolute level of expenditure, but to a group within the poor.

The main argument for targeting is that of a reduction in fiscal expenditure. This, however, is a one-sided argument that focuses only on short-term effects. As shown in Appendix 6A, there are many costs of targeting, and when all costs are taken in to account, the case for targeting becomes tenuous. Given the specific features of the Indian situation, I shall argue that it is neither desirable nor feasible to implement a policy of narrow targeting. Instead we need a system of near-universal provision.

The first argument against narrow targeting is based on the extent of food poverty and insecurity. When food insecurity is widely prevalent, the leakage from a universal programme will be small and the benefits of targeting will be limited. However, if food insecurity is low, and food subsidies need to be provided to a small section of the population then targeting can be useful. So the first question is to assess the proportion of the population that requires some kind of system of food security. If we use the food share as an indicator of food insecurity then the large majority of our population is vulnerable. As shown in Chapter 3 (Table 3.10), for the bottom 50 per cent of rural households, food shares were over 70 per cent. For the next four deciles, food shares were between 60 and 70 per cent. It is only in the top five per cent that the food share fell below 50 per cent.

By any standard, food is the most important item of expenditure for the overwhelming majority of rural households. In urban areas, the food shares were lower in every decile relative to rural areas but even here, food shares were higher than 60 per cent for the bottom six deciles and above 50 per cent for the next three deciles. If we use a generous cut-off point, namely a food share of 50 per cent, to identify the food insecure, then the top 10 per cent of the urban population and the top 5 per cent of the rural population would classify as non-eligible in 1993-94. In other words, using the food share criterion, a programme of food security should be targeted to the bottom 95 per cent of the rural population and bottom 90 per cent of the urban population. Alternatively, if a cut-off food share of 60 per cent is used (the yardstick used to identify the poor in China), then the bottom 90 per cent in rural areas and the lower 60 per cent in urban areas would have to be included. In other words, about 80 per cent of the total population would be eligible for a food security programme. By the criterion of countries such as the United States, more than 95 per cent of the population would be 'poor' (when the poor are defined as those who spend more than one-third of total expenditure on food).

To put it differently, food security in households that spend a very large proportion of their incomes on food is likely to be very sensitive to small changes in prices and incomes. From a welfare perspective, all such households should have access to some form of food security. In India, at most the top 20 per cent of the population can be excluded from systems of food security.

The second argument pertains to the weights to be attached to different types of errors of targeting. When there is mass hunger, priority must be given to welfare in terms of nutritional outcomes, and the errors of wrong exclusion and associated costs of targeting can be high in such circumstances. In other words, the weight attached to every undernourished person who is wrongly excluded from a targeted programme should be much higher than the weight attached to a rich person who benefits from the scheme. Broad targeting, as we know, is more inclusive and likely to lower the costs of wrong exclusion, and is therefore to be preferred in such a situation. The benefits to the rich can be clawed-back by means of progressive taxes.

The third and last argument in favour of near-universal coverage of PDS is based on the conceptual and practical problems of administrative targeting in a less developed country such as ours. A large part of the discussion on targeting assumes, explicitly or implicitly, that the population can be divided into 'poor' and 'non-poor' categories on the basis of income or expenditure. There are, however, serious problems when income targeting is attempted, as has been the case of Targeted PDS. First, as argued in Chapter 6, there are huge problems of measurement of incomes. When there is very tight targeting, say with a specific and low-income cut-off, errors in measurement can mean disqualification for genuinely poor persons. Secondly, there are incentives to cheat, and it is easier to distort information when there are already genuine problems of measurement. For example, when the ability to cross-check information is limited, cheating is easier. Thirdly, and this issue has not been paid sufficient attention, the use of a time-specific cut-off makes little sense when there is upward and downward income mobility. Studies of income mobility in developing countries are few because of the paucity of panel data. However, the available evidence shows that there is significant income mobility even in the lower income deciles (see Gaiha 1988). Mobility is higher in the middle of the income distribution and least at the upper end of the distribution (e.g., the top decile). To put it differently, while it is easy to identify the rich and they tend to remain rich, there is much more mobility among households in the lower income deciles. Without adequate panel data and continual re-assessment of incomes, a one-time identification of the 'poor' or target group is likely to be welfare-defeating. Further, mobility is highest in the region where a cut-off is likely to be drawn (such as in the fourth or fifth decile of incomes). This makes the selection of an appropriate cut-off extremely difficult. Fourthly, and this is a related issue, the process of defining a target group has to change in the presence of mobility. For example, while there is upward mobility among the lowest deciles, there is also downward mobility among the upper deciles. In one study from India, 13 per cent of the 'non-poor' in 1968 became 'poor' in 1970 (Gaiha 1987). In other words, there is a risk of income decline for those not presently in a position of severe deprivation. So a policy that is concerned not only with the chronically hungry but also with those vulnerable to income fluctuations, and changes in food consumption should define the target group broadly.

Finally, the lesson from Kerala is also that if a near-universal system of distribution works well it can reach poor households effectively.

TABLE 7.1 *Ration scale or entitlements, selected countries (in kg.)*

State or Country	Food grain quota per month (in kg)
Kerala	13.2 kg. per person
Andhra Pradesh: white cards	5 kg. per person (ceiling: 20/25 kg.)
Tamil Nadu	7 kg. per person (ceiling: 27 kg.)
Maharashtra	10 kg. per person (ceiling: 20/30 kg.)
Uttar Pradesh	14–18 kg. per person
Bihar	8 kg. per person
China: Beijing	15–29 kg. per adult
China: Chengdu	14 (office worker) – 25 kg. (manual labourer)
Sri Lanka	7.2 kg. per person

Source Riskin (1987) for China, Anand and Kanbur (1991) for Sri Lanka and GOI (1994b) for India.

Note The ration scales for Indian states refer to the scales prevalent before the introduction of the Targeted PDS.

The quantity supplied and adequacy of ration scale

If the system of food subsidy is to contribute significantly to household nutrition and food security, then a reasonable minimum quantity of grain needs to be distributed. The quantity distributed should bear some relation to minimum cereal requirements. According to the Indian Council of Medical Research (ICMR 1990), per capita cereal requirements amount to 135 kg. a year (or 370 gms. per person per day). PDS should aim to provide, at the very least, about half the daily cereal requirements, that is 67 kg. per person per year or 5.6 kg. a month.

Let us examine the scale of rationing under a range of schemes in relation to these norms or requirements (Table 7.1). International comparisons show that China (before 1993) and Sri Lanka (before 1980) had very generous ration quotas. In China, the quantity allocated varied with age, sex and activity of the person; there were also variations across regions. In Chengdu, for example, an office worker was allocated 14 kg. of grain a month whereas a manual worker was entitled to 25 kg. a month. In Sri Lanka, the ration scheme used to provide up to 7.2 kg. per person each month. By contrast, the ration scales are much lower in India. Before TPDS, one of the most generous ration quotas was in Uttar Pradesh but, of course, in practice, very little reached the people. Kerala has the next highest ration scale of 13.2 kg. per person per month or 158 kg. a year. This scale is adequate in a nutritional sense in that if a person bought her entire quota it would meet her total grain requirements. In practice, the per capita purchase from PDS has been about 70 kg. a year in Kerala. PDS purchases thus meet roughly half the consumption requirements of people in Kerala. In most other states the ration scale is smaller and far from adequate. Moreover, the ration entitlement has been lowered in many states after the introduction of TPDS. At the national level, only 10 kg. are now guaranteed for each poor family, that is, 2 to 3 kg. a month for each poor person.

The quantity supplied to PDS has clearly to expand if it is to be more effective. To satisfy a cereal requirement of 370 gms. per person a day for those below the poverty line, it has been calculated that an additional 32.4 million tonnes of cereals needs to be distributed in PDS (Geetha and Suryanarayana, 1993). In another study, Chandrasekhar and Sen (1996) estimated that 22 million tonnes of food grain would be needed if one-third of current per capita grain availability was to be provided to the bottom 40 per cent of the population through a food-for-work type programme.

What would be the scale of PDS if a ration of 70 kg., the achievement in Kerala, were to be provided to all hungry and undernourished house-holds? If this ration were provided to the bottom 60 per cent (say 600 million) of the population, then the annual requirement of the PDS would be 42 million tonnes (or 25 per cent of net availability). In the 1990s, particularly after 1992, the quantity of food grain distributed in PDS declined: it fell sharply from 1992 to 1995 and then recovered slightly. Thus, as argued in Chapter 6, PDS was weakened in the 1990s by means of a reduction in the quantity supplied.

I shall argue that contrary to the policies of the present government, PDS needs to be *expanded* if it is to provide minimum nutritional support to participant households. Is this feasible? For a country that produces around 200 million tonnes of food grain, surely public policy can ensure that about one-fifth is procured and distributed through PDS. This will, of course, require reform of policies of production and procurement (see below).

Thus far, we have been concerned solely with cereals but the same argument would apply to all commodities that are to be supplied in PDS. In other words, to be effective, all rationed commodities should be supplied in adequate quantity in the public distribution system.

Quality of grain

It is also important to ensure that the food grain supplied to PDS conforms to certain minimum standards of quality. There are strict norms for FCI (such as on the moisture content, extent of damaged or broken rice) that specify the nature of 'fair average quality' grain. Nevertheless, on account of various factors including non-mechanization of cleaning and weighing, poor storage, poor packaging, there is some deterioration in the quality of grain. Better quality control is thus required. At the same time, there has to be monitoring of the quality of grain between the time it leaves the FCI depots and the time of sale in fair-price shops.

Control over food prices

Since Independence, one of the key objectives of food policy and food subsidy programmes in India has been to maintain price stability and ensure that basic foods are available to the vulnerable population at reasonable prices. This goal was attained to the extent that the real price of basic cereals such as rice and wheat was kept in check, and declined through the 1970s and 1980s, and price fluctuations were lowered. Also, fluctuations in domestic prices were much lower than fluctuations in world prices, and thus the consumer in India was protected from excessive price variations. In the 1990s, however, as we have shown in Chapter 6, food prices rose rapidly and exceeded price rises in other commodities. The relative price of food commodities such as rice actually rose in the 1990s. In particular, the prices of rice and wheat in PDS were raised repeatedly in the period 1992 to 1994. In a country where the majority of the population is not adequately nourished, it is essential that governments keep a check on inflation in food prices. The erosion of real incomes of the poor via high inflation in food prices has to be reversed.

It is not easy, of course, to establish precisely what constitutes a 'reasonable' or 'affordable' price, but the price of cereals and other basic foods must bear some relation to wages, incomes and levels of poverty in society.

Production, procurement and the Food Corporation of India

Since PDS involves the distribution of food, it has to be supported by systems of procurement and storage. Policies of production and procurement have to be of a piece with policies of distribution, and specifically, an expanded PDS requires expansion of the production base and a more equitable system of procurement. We also need to examine the functioning of the Food Corporation of India (FCI), the body that implements the government's policy of procurement and storage.

Production and procurement
It is alarming that the World Bank and others are arguing that it is now appropriate to 'phase out government controls as well as procurement policies' (World Bank 1996: 40) on the grounds that India has moved from a situation of a deficit to that of surplus in grain production. This is a very short-run view. If all the hungry and undernourished consumed adequate amounts of food grain then present production would barely suffice to meet demand. One set of projections of cereal demand for 2020 show that 278 million tonnes may be demanded if per capita income grows at 3 per cent annually (Bhalla and Hazell 1997). In addition, if poverty were eliminated, cereal demand would rise to 292 million tonnes, and if the entire population were well fed, cereal demand would be 301 million tonnes (ibid.). Clearly, domestic production needs to expand rapidly to meet this demand. In other words, for supply to keep pace with future increases in demand, it is necessary to expand the production base. In particular, there is need to raise productivity and production in more backward regions and, in dry-land areas, and such progress will require appropriate producer incentives.

For a country the size of India, the goal of self-sufficiency in domestic production, contrary to the logic of structural adjustment, cannot be abandoned.[1] A reliance on imports to meet the food requirements of several hundred million persons will not only make Indian consumers vulnerable to world trade fluctuations but also undermine national sovereignty.

Further, as argued above, the quantity of food grain distributed in PDS needs to be raised if PDS is to provide minimum nutritional support to even the lowest 60 per cent of the population. An expanded PDS would require some reorientation of the system of procurement. At present,

---

[1]   See, for instance, Patnaik (1996, 1997).

procurement is highly concentrated in a few regions. In 1989–90, for example, Punjab and Haryana accounted for 23 per cent of all-India rice production and 63 per cent of rice procurement. In the case of wheat, Punjab and Haryana generated 69 per cent of the total output and nearly all of procurement. We need a scheme of procurement that ensures some equity between states and across cultivators within a state.[2] A more widespread production base with local and regional procurement can also lower the costs of procurement and distribution.[3]

Food Corporation of India
As shown in Chapter 4, total economic costs of the FCI roughly doubled between 1990–91 and 1998–99 for its operations in both rice and wheat, resulting in a growing gap between costs and sales price. Nevertheless, the ratio of economic cost to procurement price declined for wheat after 1991–92 and was more or less unchanged for rice during the 1990s. This ratio, an indicator of operational efficiency, that measures the costs of acquisition and distribution relative to the costs of purchase, shows that operational inefficiency did not worsen in the 1990s.

The nature of cost escalation showed that the fastest growing component of economic costs was the procurement price of food grain. A check on procurement prices is thus essential to rein in the total costs of the FCI. As I argued above, we still need policies of procurement and price support but they must be viewed in conjunction with costs of the FCI and costs to the consumers via raised prices in PDS. At the same time, it is obvious that costs of distribution (including freight, handling charges and overhead charges) have risen rapidly and these costs need to be controlled. There are also costs due to waste, specifically losses during transit and storage, and these must be brought down sharply.

---

[2] It is worth thinking through the scheme for equitable procurement to meet the needs of PDS that was made by Gulati and Krishnan (1975). The basic elements of their scheme were a system of graded producer levy, procurement at reasonable prices and equity in the distribution of burden across states and across farmers.

[3] By expanding the base of procurement, we could ease the strain on the system that is caused by pressures applied by the rich farmers of the states that dominate supplies to PDS. On the gains made by surplus farmers in selected north-western states in the present system of procurement, see Raghavan (1999).

Thus, without doubt, there is scope for streamlining operations and lowering the operational costs of the FCI. In this context, the recommend-ations made by the Bureau of Industrial Costs and Prices (BICP1991) such as deferred procurement and decentralized storage should be discussed seriously. The BICP report made many detailed recommendations that dealt with corporate structure (the need for accountability, for delegation of powers), with quality control (the quality of FCI mills, improved weighing facilities), and with corruption (the need for better vigilance, security at depots), to mention a few. Implementing these suggestions requires not only greater autonomy for the FCI but also major organiz-ational changes.

Waste and mismanagement, however, does not justify the demand made by reformers that the FCI be privatized. A recent World Bank study recommended that the FCI 'go out of the operations of procurement and supply to the PDS' (World Bank 1996: 77). The assumption underlying this argument is that private trade is more efficient than the FCI, an assumption that is driven by ideological considerations and not empirical evidence. The detailed and critical evaluation undertaken by the BICP concluded that, 'while the overall assessment of FCI operations in managing the food economy is satisfactory, its performance can be substantially improved' (BICP 1991: 45). We need to improve the functioning of the FCI by building on its strengths (such as its impressive all-India distribution network) rather than dismantling it along the lines suggested by the World Bank.

Finally, it was shown that a growing share of the total costs of the FCI was spent on maintaining buffer stocks. At the same time, as pointed out in Chapter 6, the government has been holding 'excess stocks', that is, quantities in surplus of the buffer stock requirements. The FCI and the government could thus save resources – and feed hungry people – if the existing surplus stocks were distributed free of cost or provided through means such as Food-for-Work programmes. The cost of maintaining large excess stocks is high, and the carrying costs incurred by the FCI would fall if these stocks were reduced.

To sum up, we need to broaden the base of production and this should be accompanied by new and more diversified procurement. The operational costs of distribution and storage by the FCI must be kept in control by means such as greater transparency and accountability in day-to-day functioning. In short, there needs to be a unity of policy design with respect to procurement and distribution.

Administration and functioning of the food delivery system

In most parts of the country, to be effective, the administration and management of PDS need major overhaul. Much of the unevenness in the utilization of PDS in different parts of the country and the associated failure to reach some of the poorest households and regions can be attributed to administrative failure. The food delivery network needs to be strengthened and administered in a non-corrupt and efficient manner for the poor to have access to PDS. Some specific suggestions follow.

The general functioning of ration shops needs to be improved. Ration shops should be open for reasonable number of hours each day or at regular intervals. More shops are needed in areas of high population density, such as urban slums, to prevent long queues and overcrowding. More shops are also needed in remote rural areas. Households should be permitted to purchase their entitlements in several instalments (and not just once or twice a month). The minimum purchase requirement should be kept low so as to enable persons such as daily wage earners to buy their requirements in small quantities. In many parts of the country, the low utilization of PDS is on account of the poverty of households, and specifically, the lack of cash to make a bulk purchase of 10 or 20 kg. on the few days of the month that commodities are available in the ration store. Ration commodities should be made available on a regular basis and not just on a few days each month. A stable supply of commodities in fair-price shops is essential if the ration shop is to be accessible to all households.

Goods should conform to certain quality standards. An oft-heard complaint from consumers is that grain in ration shops is soiled, full of stones, smelly and generally of low quality. It is important to recall that in Kerala, where ration purchases are frequent and regular among a large section of the population, complaints about quality were not very serious (Koshy et al. 1989). In fact, the availability of unadulterated items was one of the reasons given for purchases from the ration shop (ibid.). Another important factor is the weights and measures used for sale of commodities and we need to ensure that consumers are not cheated by short-weighing. To bring in greater accountability, consumers must have adequate information about the availability of commodities, about their entitlements, and about prices. When people are aware and informed, they can act as a check on malpractice in the administration of ration shops.

Good administration of the delivery system requires checks and balances not just at the level of the ration shop but at every level of administration. One suggestion in this regard is to assign the task of delivery of PDS to Panchayati Raj Institutions. Decentralization is the right direction to go, as it is likely to improve control and accountability of the delivery system. Decentralization will also allow for the possibility of local variations in the system of food subsidies and food delivery. The precondition, however, is the presence of genuine democratic panchayats. Today, the nature and composition of panchayats is very different in states such as West Bengal, where rudimentary land reform has been implemented and where local power structures have been altered, and states such as Bihar, where backward agrarian relations continue to dominate rural society. In West Bengal, traditionally deprived communities now have a voice in the functioning of the panchayat institutions. In such cases, the panchayats may be expected to ensure that the delivery system better meets the needs of the poor. Without genuine land reform and changes in village social and power relations, it is difficult to ensure genuine democracy in panchayat institutions. In cases where members of the traditional land-holding hierarchy of a village dominate the panchayat, the control of panchayats over delivery is not going to change the working of PDS.

Employment and other welfare programmes

Some of the poorest households are unable to utilize PDS because they lack the income to buy food. For such households, employment or other welfare programmes (such as pensions for senior citizens) are required to enable them to buy minimum quantities of food. In the discussion on 'reform' of PDS, it is often suggested that the resources withdrawn from PDS be allocated to other welfare programmes such as employment programmes or nutrition programmes (e.g. Parikh 1994). In other words, employment programmes are viewed as substitutes for food distribution through PDS. A related suggestion has been to restrict the benefits of PDS to participants of other welfare programmes such as employment programmes (World Bank 1996). In short, linking PDS to employment schemes, it is suggested, can improve targeting and delivery. I shall argue that employment and other social security programmes should be comple-

TABLE 7.2 *Alternative proposals to reform the PDS*

Orthodox reformers	Alternative
Narrow targeting or target to the very poor; Use income to identify the poor and very poor (below 75 per cent of poverty line).	Broad targeting or target to 80-95 % of population; use food share as indicator of poverty. Prefer near-universal PDS.
Introduce Food Stamps, and reduce the value of the food subsidy.	Keep rations. Ensure that ration scale provides a reasonable quantity of food. Stamps are complicated administratively and do not protect against inflation.
Remove restrictions on grain trade; privatize FCI; and end procurement policy.	Reorient production and procurement policies. Expand production base; Extend procurement to all regions; Lower costs of FCI by greater autonomy.
Increasing role of market determined prices.	Keep food prices in control.
Administrative reform; use panchayat institutions for targeting and delivery.	Administrative reform of various kinds including greater decentralization.
Link PDS with other welfare programmes like employment programmes as a means of targeting. Allocate funds from the PDS to other welfare programmes.	Expand employment and other welfare programmes but they should complement and not substitute the PDS.

Note: The orthodox view is represented here by suggestions in World Bank (1996).

mentary to PDS and not seen as a way of restricting food distribution only to households participating in employment or other welfare programmes.

Concluding remarks

In this chapter, I outlined the main features of a strategy to strengthen PDS. The first issue discussed was that of coverage. I argued in favour of universal or near-universal coverage on the grounds that the costs of targeting are high in a country such as ours where a large majority of the population is vulnerable to food deprivation. By the criterion of the food share, even with a high cut off level, a food share of 60 per cent, 90 per cent of rural households and 60 per cent of urban households would be eligible for programmes of food security. The conceptual case for broad and universal coverage of PDS is fortified by the immense practical problems of administrative targeting based on criteria such as income poverty.

Secondly, to be effective, the quantity of food grain distributed in PDS needs to be expanded. The ration scale should bear some relation to the norm for minimum cereal requirements. I argued that PDS should attempt to provide about 70 kg. of grain per annum – that is, the Kerala achievement and half the cereal requirements of a person. At the same time, the quality of food grain should conform to certain norms.

Thirdly, a check on the prices of basic foods is an essential component of any strategy of food security. The erosion of real incomes in recent years through high inflation in food prices must be controlled.

Fourthly, policies of production, procurement and storage have to be of a piece with policies of distribution. This requires continued emphasis on self-sufficiency in food production and an expansion of the production base. It also requires a revamping of the system of procurement with more diversified procurement. Lastly, the costs of operation of the FCI, the organization responsible for procurement, storage and distribution, need to be lowered. At the same time, it should be recognized that a major component of the rise in costs, procurement price, is a variable outside the control of the FCI.

Fifthly, improvements in the administration of fair-price shops are imperative for the poor to have access to PDS. Decentralization of some functions to the local level, to democratically elected panchayats, is possibly the right direction to go, and can help improve administration and monitoring of the working of PDS.

Finally, a major factor limiting the access of the poor to PDS is inadequacy of purchasing power. So programmes of employment generation and other welfare programmes are measures complementary to PDS and need to be augmented.

With these measures, it is feasible to make PDS an effective measure of food security.

eight

Conclusions

Food security is achieved when all people, at all times, have physical and economic access to sufficient, safe and nutritious food to meet their dietary needs and food preferences for an active life.

Rome Declaration on World Food Security
World Food Summit 1996

This monograph attempted an assessment of the system of public distribution of food in India, the Public Distribution System (PDS), with a special focus on the changes that have occurred with the introduction of programmes of structural adjustment. This chapter brings together the main findings of the analysis.

The main objectives of PDS have been to provide rations during situations of scarcity, to maintain stable prices, to control private trade, and to improve the well-being of the poor by the provision of basic foods and other essential commodities at reasonable prices (Chapter 2). PDS is now sixty years old. Begun in 1939 as a war-time rationing measure, PDS was converted into a universal welfare programme in the 1960s and expanded through the 1970s and 80s.

The evidence for the continuing need for more and better systems of food security is the current state of food consumption and nutrition among the Indian population. Food deprivation and poverty persist on a mass scale in India today. By the criterion of the official poverty line, a level of expenditure that is extremely low, 320 million people (or 36 per cent of the population) were poor in 1993–94. Available evidence shows that the number of poor persons rose by another 28 million between 1993–94 and 1997 (Chapter 3).

The average consumption of cereals, the major source of energy, has fallen over time. In rural India, for instance, the average calorie intake fell from 2,221 Kcal in 1983 to 2,153 Kcal in 1993–94. In 1993–94, 80 per cent of households, on average, did not get the recommended intake of calories a day. Inadequate calorie intake is compounded by specific deficiencies of major micronutrients such as vitamin A and iron. In most states, the vitamin A intake was inadequate in 90 per cent of households surveyed. The low and inadequate intake of food is reflected in nutritional outcomes: as many as 50 per cent of adults and 55 per cent of children suffer undernutrition. Lastly, food expenditure is the major component of the family budget for the large majority of households: food expenditure accounted for more than 50 per cent of household expenditure among 95 per cent of rural households and 80 per cent of urban households. If the criterion used in the United States for identifying the poor for food stamps – that is, a household that spends more than one-third of its income on food – were used in India, more than 95 per cent of households in India would be identified as poor (Chapter 3). Food security is thus needed not only for those below the 'poverty line' defined by the government, but also for those who are vulnerable to food deprivation.

The persistence of and vulnerability to hunger and malnutrition on a mass scale is the fundamental justification for maintaining and strengthening a system of food distribution such as PDS. A striking feature of the functioning of PDS is the diversity across states, with the Kerala having the most effective and extensive system both in terms of coverage or participation and in terms of quantity of food grain distributed (Chapter 4). The NSS survey for 1986–87 showed that only two per cent of the population of Bihar utilized the fair-price shop for buying cereals as compared to 98 per cent in Kerala. Similarly, in terms of quantities, in 1998, the per capita annual supply of food grain from PDS was 67 kg. in

Kerala and 9.5 kg. in Bihar. An important observation that emerged from the review of PDS in different states was that access by the poor to PDS was closely tied to the nature of access and coverage for the entire population. In states with high coverage and an effective distribution network (such as Kerala and, to some extent, Andhra Pradesh), the poor utilized PDS more than the rich. In states with an inefficient and ineffective distribution network (such as Uttar Pradesh and Bihar), PDS reached neither the poor nor the rich. In Kerala, for instance, low-income households bought 71 per cent of their rice entitlements from PDS whereas high-income households purchased only 6 per cent of their entitlement from the system.

Another failing of the system is in the sphere of administration. Ineffective and corrupt administrative practices have weakened, to the point of destruction in some states, the system of delivery. The Government of India meets the entire operational deficit of the Food Corporation of India (FCI), the organization responsible for procurement, storage and distribution of food grain. With respect to the cost structure and changes in operational costs of the FCI, the share of subsidy incurred on buffer stock operations has risen sharply while the share spent on distribution (that is, the consumer subsidy) has fallen over time. Secondly, the costs of operation of the FCI have risen rapidly in the 1990s. However, a critical factor in this increase has been the rise in procurement prices, a variable outside the control of the FCI. Thirdly, despite the absolute increase in operational costs, the ratio of economic cost to procurement price (a measure of the costs under the control of the FCI) has declined for wheat and remained unchanged for rice in recent years. This indicates that the operational efficiency of the FCI, and worsening of operational efficiency, is not the main contributor to the rise in the subsidy bill in the 1990s (Chapter 4).

A short account of the working of PDS in Kerala demonstrated that it is possible to provide nutritional support to a large part of the population through a network of fair-price shops. Kerala is unique for having achieved a near-universal coverage of the population, for the sizeable quantity of grain provided per person in the state (around one-half of recommended intake), and for the relatively smooth administration of the system. An important element in Kerala's history of PDS is the strong people's movement for food, which was responsible both for the initial introduction of rationing, and which has put continual pressure on the political system to sustain the system of public delivery of food.

There was no clear correspondence between the effectiveness of PDS and the level of income or extent of poverty in a state (Chapter 4). We argued that the wide differences in the coverage and functioning of PDS across states were related to differences in the politics of different state governments. While the central government is responsible for the overall policy of price support, procurement, storage and distribution, state governments are responsible for implementation of PDS and can set some key parameters of the system, such as entitlements, prices and coverage. The differences in the functioning of PDS thus reflect differences in the commitment of state governments to welfare policy and specifically the commitment to the provision of cheap and adequate food to the mass of the population through PDS.

The initiation of programmes of orthodox structural adjustment in a vast number of developing countries has adversely affected programmes of food security. Case studies of five countries, namely Mexico, Sri Lanka, Jamaica, Tunisia and Zambia, showed that the crucial feature of 'structural adjustment' in these countries was a steep reduction in food subsidies (Chapter 5). The cut back in food subsidy was implemented by means of targeting and the introduction of new schemes such as food stamps. When food subsidies were cut, inflation in food prices soared. As food stamps are not fully indexed to inflation, the real value of the subsidy eroded rapidly when food prices rose. Targeting subsidized food was associated with a rise in the numbers of poor persons completely excluded from the system of food subsidies. Structural adjustment thus reduced food consumption and nutrition among vulnerable populations. As was observed in the context of Sri Lanka, 'the burden of real cuts in the food subsidy budget' fell 'disproportionately on the poor' (Anand and Kanbur 1991: 80).

In India, too, there have been major changes in policy in the post-1991 period of liberalization and these have led towards a further dismantling of the delivery system, with serious implications for food security among the poorest of households (Chapter 6). Although policies of structural adjustment are driven by the necessity of reducing the 'burden of subsidy', we found that the ratio of the central government's food subsidy to GDP has been more or less unchanged over the last twenty years. The ratio of food subsidy to GDP averaged 0.4 per cent over the last thirty years. Nevertheless, the Government of India is now committed to reducing food subsidies. One means of weakening of PDS has been the high inflation in food prices, thus undermining the objective of keeping food prices low and affordable. After a steady decline for over two decades, there was a sharp rise in the relative price of rice, and to a lesser extent wheat, in the 1990s. The index of the price of rice relative to the wholesale price index rose to 111 in 1997 when indexed at 100 in 1981–82. Furthermore, inflation in the prices of rice and wheat in PDS exceeded inflation in other price and cost of living indices. Between 1991 and 1994, while the index of wholesale prices rose 44 per cent, the central issue price of wheat rose 72 per cent and that of the common variety of rice rose 86 per cent. Not surprisingly, the gap between prices of commodities in fair-price shops and in the open market has narrowed. At the same time, the quantity of food supplied to PDS declined. In 1991, 20.8 million tones of rice and wheat were distributed through the PDS network; the quantity fell to 14 million tonnes in 1994. While the offtake of cereals from the public distribution system fell, stocks of rice and wheat surpassed minimum requirements by large margins. Since 1993, actual stocks have been consistently higher than the norm in every quarter. Thus the post-1991 period witnessed the irrational phenomenon of rising food stocks on the one hand, and falling food offtake from the PDS on the other hand.

Lastly, guided by the doctrines of orthodox structural adjustment, public policy in the sphere of food distribution has attempted to cut back coverage and consumption by means of introducing narrow targeting and a denial of the principle of universal transfers (Chapter 6). Targeted PDS introduced in 1997 is the thin edge of the wedge: it is the first step towards abandoning food security by means of the system of public distribution of food. Contrary to popular perceptions, targeting does not mean more benefits for the poor. Targeting raises the error of wrongly excluding the poor and lowers the error of wrongly including the rich. There are thus costs attached to targeting, particularly in terms of a fall in welfare for the poor. The choice between universal and targeted transfers, as argued in Appendix 6A, becomes less clear-cut when the costs of targeting are taken account of, and in the long-run, universal transfers are preferable to targeted transfers in a situation such as the one in India. The specific scheme for targeting introduced in India has attempted to classify households into 'poor' and 'non-poor' categories on the basis of the official poverty line. We argued that targeting based on an income criterion is extremely difficult to administer in a country like ours, and is likely to result in large targeting errors. Another major change introduced in TPDS has been to fix entitlements, on a per family – rather than per capita – basis at the meagre level of 10 kg. per month for 'poor' households. The 'non-poor' population is no longer guaranteed an entitlement of food grain from PDS. The new principle of allocation of food grain penalizes states that were distributing a larger quantity of food than others through PDS. After the introduction of TPDS, with the exception of Kerala, all the states at the top of the all-India ranking in terms of quantity of grain distributed have seen their share fall. Lastly, given the changes in prices (lower prices for 'below-poverty-line' allocations and significantly higher prices for 'above-poverty-line' allocations) and entitlements, the cost of a minimum basket of food is likely to have risen for the typical low-income family (Chapter 6).

Given the problems with PDS as it is today, and the need to have an effective system of food security, in Chapter 7, I outlined certain key elements of a strategy for reform of PDS. The main suggestions were the following.

1. Given the scale of chronic hunger in India, I argued in favour of universal or near-universal provision. If the food share is used to identify persons vulnerable to food insecurity, the vast majority of our population becomes eligible for a programme such as PDS. In practical terms, it will be easier to provide universal benefits and then claw-back benefits from the rich via other means such as taxes.

2. An adequate quantity of grain needs to be distributed to make a sizeable contribution to household food security. The delivery system should be ensured of a regular and adequate supply of all rationed commodities.

3. Food prices need to be kept in check and prices of commodities supplied in PDS should be reasonable and affordable by the poor.

4. A strong and effective system of procurement needs to be maintained to meet the requirements of an effective and expanded PDS. Clearly, procurement has to be backed by production, and this entails the pursuit of the goal of self-sufficiency in production. Policies of

production, procurement, storage and distribution need to be planned in conjunction.

5. Major improvements are needed in the administration of PDS to ensure a non-corrupt and efficient delivery system. Decentralization can improve the working of the delivery system.

6. Programmes of employment generation and other social security programmes are complementary to PDS and need to be expanded in order to provide purchasing power to some of the poorest households.

7. A lesson from Kerala, the only state in India with a comprehensive and well functioning public distribution system, is that strong political support and political awareness is essential for establishing and maintaining an effective system of food security.

To fulfil the promise made in the Rome Declaration on World Food Security, the Government of India needs to expand and strengthen programmes of food security, and reform the public distribution system so as to make it an effective means of providing nutritional support to the majority of our population.

Bibliography

Ahluwalia, D., 1993, 'Public Distribution of Food in India: Coverage, Targeting and Leakages', *Food Policy*, 18, 1, February.

Anand, S. and C. Harris, 1990, 'Food and Standard of Living: An Analysis Based on Sri Lankan Data', in J. Dreze and A. Sen (eds.) *The Political Economy of Hunger*, volume 1, Oxford: Clarendon Press.

Anand, S. and S.M. Ravi Kanbur, 1991, 'Public Policy and Basic Needs Provision: Intervention and Achievement in Sri Lanka', in J. Dreze and A. Sen (eds.) *The Political Economy of Hunger*, volume 3, Oxford: Clarendon Press.

Appendini, K., 1997, 'Seguridad alimentaria en un contexto vulnerable: el sistema maiz-tortilla', Simposio trinacional de investigacion: el TLC y la agricultura, Texas, San Antonio, 1–2 November.

Bapna, S.L., 1990, 'Food Security Through the PDS: The Indian Experience' in D.S. Tyagi and V.S. Vyas (eds.) *Increasing Access to Food: The Asian Experience*, Sage Publications.

Besley, T. and R. Kanbur, 1988, 'Food Subsidies and Poverty Alleviation', *Economic Journal*, 98, pp. 701–19.

———, 1993, 'The Principles of Targeting' in Lipton and van der Gaag 1993.

Bhalla, G.S., 1994, 'Policy for Food Security in India', in Bhalla (ed.).

——— (ed.), 1994, *Economic Liberalization and Indian Agriculture*, New Delhi: Institute for Studies in Industrial Development.

———, and P. Hazell, 1997, 'Foodgrains Demand in India to 2020: A Preliminary Exercise', *Economic and Political Weekly*, 23, 52, December 27, pp. A 150–54.

Bhagwati, J. and T.N. Srinivasan, 1993, *India's Economic Reforms*, Government of India, Ministry of Finance.

Boyd, D., 1988, 'The Impact of Adjustment Polices on Vulnerable Groups: The Case of Jamaica' in G.A. Cornia, R. Jolly and F. Stewart (eds.) *Adjustment with a Human Face*, volume 2, Oxford: Clarendon Press.

Brachet-Marquez, V. and M.S. Sherraden, 1994, 'Political Change and the Welfare State: The Case of Health and Food Policies in Mexico', *World Development*, 22, 9, pp. 1295–1312.

Braun, J. von, H. Bouis, S. Kumar and R. Pandya-Lorch, 1992, 'Improving Food Security of the Poor: Concept, Policy and Programs', IFPRI, Washington, D.C.

Bureau of Industrial Costs and Prices (BICP), 1991, *Report on the Operations of the Food Corporation of India*, New Delhi.

Burgess, R. and N. Stern, 1991, 'Social Security in Developing Countries: What, Why, Who and How?' in Ahmad, E. et al., *Social Security in Developing Countries*, Oxford: Clarendon Press.

Chandrasekhar, C.P. and J. Ghosh, 1997, 'Targeted Public Distribution System: Is it Getting More Food to the Poor?', *Business Line*, July 22.

Chandrasekhar, C.P. and A. Sen, 1996, 'Statistical Truths, Economic Reform and Poverty' *Frontline*, February 23.

Cornia, G.A. and F. Stewart, 1993, 'Two Errors of Targeting', *Journal of International Development*, 5, 5, pp. 459–90.

Damodaran, H., 1999, 'Wheat offtake shows no signs of pick-up', *Business Line*, November 17.

Dantwala, M., 1976, 'Agricultural Policy in India since Independence', *Indian Journal of Agricultural Economics*, 31, 4.

Dreze, J. and A. Sen, 1989, *Hunger and Public Action*, Oxford: Clarendon Press.

Dreze, J., P. Lanjouw and N. Stern, 1998, 'Economic Development in Palanpur 1957–1993, in Lanjouw and Stern 1998.

Edirisinghe, N., 1987, *The Food Stamp Scheme in Sri Lanka: Costs, Benefits and Options for Modification*, IFPRI Research Report 58.

———, 1988, 'Food Subsidy Changes in Sri Lanka: The Short-Run Effect on the Poor' in Pinstrup-Andersen (ed.), pp. 253–66.

Food and Agricultural Organisation (FAO), 1989, 'Effects of Stabilization and Structural Adjustment Programmes on Food Security', Economic and Social Development Paper 89, Rome.

Gaiha 1988, 'Income Mobility in Rural India, *Economic Development and Cultural Change*, 36, 2, January, pp. 279–302.

Geetha, S. and M.H. Suryanarayana, 1993, 'Revamping PDS: Some Issues and Implications', *Economic and Political Weekly*, October 9, pp. 2207–13.

George, P.S., 1979, 'Public Distribution of Foodgrains in Kerala, Income Distribution Implications and Effectivenes', IFPRI, Research Report 7, March.

Goodin, R.E. and J. Le Grand, 1987, *Not Only the Poor: The Middle Classes and the Welfare State*, London: Allen and Unwin.

Government of India, 1991, *Annual Report 1990–91*, Ministry of Food and Civil Supplies, Department of Civil Supplies.

———, 1992, *Economic Survey*, Ministry of Finance.

———, 1993a, *National Policy on Public Distribution System, Report of the Committee of Ministers*, Ministry of Civil Supplies, Consumer Affairs and Public Distribution, New Delhi.

———, 1993b, *Bulletin on Food Statistics 1992–1993*, Ministry of Agriculture, Directorate of Economics and Statistics, New Delhi.

———, 1994a, *Economic Survey 1993–94*, Ministry of Finance.

———, 1994b, *Annual Report 1993–94*, Ministry of Civil Supplies.

———, 1997, *Focus on the Poor*, Ministry of Civil Supplies, Consumer Affairs and Public Distribution, New Delhi.

Government of Maharashtra, *Economic Survey of Maharashtra*, Directorate of Economics and Statistics, Bombay, different years.

Grosh, M.E., 1992, 'The Jamaican Food Stamps Programme', *Food Policy*, 17, 1.

Gulati, A., P. Sharma and S. Kahkonen, 1997, The Food Corporation of India: Successes and Failures in Indian Foodgrain Marketing', paper presented at the Conference, Agriculture and Rural Reform, Institutions and Economic Policy, January 21–22, Indian Institute of Management, Calcutta.

Gulati, I.S. and T.N. Krishnan, 1975, 'Public Distribution and Procurement of Foodgrains: A Proposal', *Economic and Political Weekly*, 10, 21, May 24, pp. 829–42.

Gupta, S.P., 1999, 'Globalization, Economic Reforms and the Role of Labour', Society for Economic and Social Transition, New Delhi.

Handa, S. and D. King, 1997, 'Structural Adjustment Policies, Income Distribution and Poverty: A Review of the Jamaican Experience', *World Development*, 25, 6, June.

Herring, R.J., 1987, 'The Dependent Welfare State: Nutrition, Entitlements and Exchange in Sri Lanka' in W.L. Hollist and F.L. Tullis (eds.) *Pursuing Food Security*, Lynne Riennen.

Howes, S. and S. Jha, 1992, 'Urban Bias in the Indian Public Distribution System', *Economic and Political Weekly*, May 9, pp. 1022–30.

Indian Council of Medical Research (ICMR), 1990, *Nutrient Requirements and Recommended Dietary Allowances for Indian* (Report of the Expert Group of the ICMR).

Indrakant, S., 1995, 'Food Security and Public Distribution System in Andhra Pradesh', Workshop on Food Security and Public Distribution System in India, Planning Commission, New Delhi, April.

International Institute of Population Sciences (IIPS), 1995, *National Family Health Survey 1992–93: India*, Bombay.

Jayawardena, L., A. Maasland and P.N. Radhakrishnan, 1988, *Stabilization and Adjustment Policies and Programmes: Country Study 15, Sri Lanka*, WIDER, Helsinki.

Jha, S., 1992, 'Consumer Subsidies in India: Is Targeting Effective?', *Development and Change*, 23, 4, pp. 101–28.

Jones, S., 1994, 'Structural Adjustment in Zambia' in Willem van der Geest (ed.), *Negotiating Structural Adjustment in Africa*, London: UNDP and James Currey.

Kannan, K.P., 1995, 'Declining Incidence of Rural Poverty in Kerala', *Economic and Political Weekly*, 30, 41–42, October 14–21, pp. 2651–62.

Koshy, A., A.A. Gopalakrishnan, V. Vijayachandran and N.K. Jayakumar, 1989, *Report of the Study on Evaluation of the Public Distribution System in Kerala*, Trivandrum: Centre for Management Development.

Kuhn, B.A., P.A. Dunn, D. Smallwood, K. Hanson, J. Blaylock and S. Vogel, 1996, 'The Food Stamp Program and Welfare Reform', *Journal of Economic Perspectives*, 10, 2, Spring, pp. 189–98.

Kumar, Shubh K., 1979, 'Impact of Subsidized Rice on Food Consumption and Nutrition in Kerala', IFPRI, Research Report 5.

Kumar, Shubh K., 1988, 'Design, Income Distribution and Consumption Effects of Maize Pricing Policies in Zambia' in Pinstrup-Andersen 1988.

Lanjouw, P. and N. Stern (eds.), 1998, *Economic Development in Palanpur over Five Decades*, Delhi: Oxford University Press.

Li Shi, 1999, 'Urban Poverty Research in China: Some Methodological Issues', paper prepared for the International Roundtable on Urban Poverty Research, Nha Trang, Vietnam, December 13–15.

Lipton, M. and J. van der Gaag (eds.), 1993, *Including the Poor*, The World Bank, Washington, D.C.

Lipton, M. and M. Ravallion, 1995, 'Poverty and Policy' in J. Behrman and T.N. Srinivasan (eds.) *Handbook of Development Economics*, volume III, pp. 2551–657, Elsevier Science B.V.

Lustig, N., 1992, *Mexico: The Remaking of an Economy*, Brookings Institution, Washington, D.C.

Mahendra Dev, S. and M.H. Suryanarayana, 1991, 'Is PDS Urban-Biased and Pro-Rich: An Evaluation', *Economic and Political Weekly*, October 12, 26, 41, pp. 2357–66.

Malhotra, R., 1997, 'Incidence of Poverty in India: Towards a Consensus on Estimating the Poor', *Indian Journal of Labour Economics*, 40, 1, January–March.

Moghe, K., 1997, 'Redefining the Poor', *Frontline*, 14, 21, October 31.

Mooij, Jos, 1998, 'Real Targeting: The Case of Food Distribution in India', Institute of Social Studies', Working Paper Series no. 276.

———, 1999, *Food Policy and the Indian States, The PDS in South India*, New Delhi: Oxford University Press.

Mwanza, A.M., N. Mwamba and E. Kakuwa, 1992, 'The Structural Adjustment Programme in Zambia: Lessons from Experience' in A.M. Mwanza et al. (eds.) *Structural Adjustment Programmes in SADC*, Harare: SAPES Books.

National Nutrition Monitoring Bureau, 1993, *Nutritional Status of Rural Population, Report of NNMB Surveys (1991–92)*, Hyderabad.

National Nutrition Monitoring Bureau, 1996, *Nutritional Status of Rural Population, Report of NNMB Surveys*, Hyderabad.

National Sample Survey Organization, 1990, 'Utilization of Public Distribution System: NSS 42nd round (July 1986–June 1987)', *Sarvekshana*, 13, 4 (43).

———, 1997a, *Consumption of Some Important Commodities in India*, NSS 50th Round 1993–94.

———, 1997b, 'A Note on Nutritional Intake in India: NSS 50th Round (July 1993 to June 1994)', *Sarvekshana*, volume XXI, no. 2, 73rd Issue, October–December.

Nayyar, D. and A. Sen, 1994, 'International Trade and the Agricultural Sector' *Economic and Political Weekly*, May 14.

Pal, S., D.K. Bahl and Mruthyunjaya, 1993, 'Government Interventions in Foodgrain Markets', *Food Policy*, 18, 5, October.

Parikh, K., 1994, 'Who Gets How Much from PDS: How Effectively Does it Reach the Poor?', *Sarvekshana*, January–March.

Patnaik, U., 1996, 'Export-Oriented Agriculture and Food Security in Developing Countries and India', *Economic and Political Weekly*, Special No., September, pp. 2429–49.

Patnaik, U., 1997, 'Political Economy of State Intervention in Food Economy', *Economic and Political Weekly*, May 24.

Pearce, R., 1991, 'Urban Food Subsidies in the Context of Adjustment: The Case of Zambia', *Food Policy*, 16, 6, December, pp. 436–50.

———, 1994, 'Food Consumption and Adjustment in Zambia' in W. van der Geest (ed.), *Negotiating Structural Adjustment in Africa*, London: UNDP and James Currey.

Pfefferman, G.P. and C.C. Griffin, 1989, *Nutrition and Health Programs in Latin America, Targeting Social Expenditures*, IBRD, Washington, D.C.

Pinstrup-Andersen, P., 1993, 'The Role of Food-Linked Income Transfers in Efforts to Alleviate Malnutrition' in M. Lipton and van der Gaag (eds.).

———, M. Jaramillo and F. S. Stewart, 1991, 'The Impact on Government Expenditure', in G.A. Corma, R. Jolly and F. Stewart (eds.), *Adjustment with a Human Face*, volume 1, Oxford: Clarendon Press.

———, and R. Pandya-Lorch, 1994, 'Poverty and Income Distribution Aspects of Changing Food and Agriculture Policies during Structural Adjustment' in F. Heidhues and B. Knorr (eds.), *Food and Agricultural Policies under Structural Adjustment*, Peter Lang.

Radhakrishna, R., 1996, 'Food Trends, Public Distribution and Food Security Concerns', *Indian Journal of Agricultural Economics*, 51, nos. 1 and 2, pp. 168–83.

Radwan, S., V. Jamal and A. Ghose, 1991, *Tunisia, Rural Labour and Structural Transformation*, London and New York: Routledge.

Ramachandran, V.K., 1996, 'Kerala's Development Achievements: A Review', in J. Dreze and Amartya Sen (eds.), *Indian Development: Selected Regional Perspectives*, Oxford University Press.

———, 1998, Interview with E.M.S. Namboodiripad, *Frontline*, May.

Riskin, C., 1987, 'Feeding China: The Experience Since 1949' WIDER Working Paper WP 27, November, Helsinki.

Rogers, B.L., 1988, 'Design and Implementation Considerations for Consumer-Oriented Food Subsidies' in Pinstrup-Andersen (ed.).

Rome Declaration on Food Security, 1996, *Population and Development Review*, 22, 4.

Sahn, D.E., 1987, 'Changes in the Living Standards of the Poor in Sri Lanka During a Period of Macroeconomic Restructuring', *World Development*, 15, 6, pp. 809–30.

Sen, A., 1992, 'Poverty Alleviation: Targeting versus Universalization', Convocation Address at Management Development Institute, Gurgaon, India, July 3.

———, 1995, 'The Political Economy of Targeting' in van de Walle and Nead (eds.), pp. 11–24.

Shariff, A. and A.C. Mallick, 1999, 'Dynamics of Food Intake and Nutrition by Expenditure Class in India', *Economic and Political Weekly*, 34, 27, July 3.

Shetty, P.S. and W.P.T. James, 1994, 'Body Mass Index, A Measure of Chronic Energy Deficiency in Adults', FAO, Food and Nutrition Paper, 6, Rome.

Sivaswamy, K.G. et al., 1946, 'Food Control and Nutrition Surveys, Malabar and South Kanara', Servindia Kerala Relief Centre, Madras.

Srinivasan, T.N. and P.K. Bardhan, 1974, *Poverty and Income Distribution in India*, Statistical Publishing Society, Calcutta.

Subramanian, V., 1975, *Parched Earth, The Maharashtra Drought 1970–73*, Bombay: Orient Longman.

Suryanarayana, M. H., 1995a, 'Growth, Poverty and Levels of Living; Hypotheses, Methods and Policy', *Journal of Indian School of Political Economy*, 7, 2, April–June.

———, 1995b, 'Some Experiments with Food Stamps: A Survey', *Economic and Political Weekly*, December 30, pp. A 151–59.

———, 1996, 'Food Security and Calorie Adequacy across States: Implications for Reform', *Journal of Indian School of Political Economy*, 8, 2, April–June.

———, 1997, 'Food Policies: Need for an Integrated Perspective', *Productivity*, 38, 2, July–September.

Swaminathan, M., 1995, 'Revamped Public Distribution System: A Field Report from Maharashtra', *Economic and Political Weekly*, September 9.

———, 1996, 'Structural Adjustment, Food Security and the System of Public Distribution of Food', *Economic and Political Weekly*, June 29, pp 1665-1627.

———, 1999, 'Understanding the Costs of the Food Corporation of India', *Economic and Political Weekly*, December 25–31.

———, 2000, 'Consumer Food Subsidies in India: Proposals for Reform', *Journal of Peasant Studies*, (forthcoming).

———, and V. K. Ramachandran, 1999 'New Data on Calorie Intakes', *Frontline*, March 12.

Taylor, L., 1988, *Varieties of Stabilization Experience: Towards Sensible*

Macroeconomics in the Third World, Oxford: Clarendon Press.

————, 1991, 'Stabilization and Adjustment' in UNDP, Stabilization and Adjustment, New York.

————, and U. Pieper, 1996, 'Reconciling Economic Reform and Sustainable Human Development: Social Consequences of Neo-Liberalism', UNDP, Office of Development Studies, Discussion Paper Series, 2.

Tendulkar, S.D., K. Sundaram and L.R. Jain, 1993, 'Poverty in India, 1970–71 to 1988–89' ARTEP Working Papers, International Labour Office, New Delhi.

Tuck, L. and K. Lindert, 1996, *From Universal Food Subsidies to a Self-Targeted Program: A Case Study in Tunisian Reform,* World Bank Discussion Paper No. 351, Washington D.C.

Tyagi, D.S., 1990, 'Increasing Access to Food through Interaction of Price and Technology Policies, The Indian Experience' in Tyagi and Vyas 1990.

————, and V.S. Vyas (eds.), 1990, *Increasing Access to Food: The Asian Experience,* Sage Publications.

Van de Walle, D., 1995, 'Incidence and Targeting: An Overview of Implications for Research and Policy' in van de Walle and Nead (eds.), pp. 585–619.

————, and K. Nead (eds.), 1995, *Public Spending and the Poor, Theory and Evidence,* A World Bank Book, John Hopkins University Press.

Venugopal, K.R., 1992, *Deliverance from Hunger: The Public Distribution System in India,* Sage Publications.

Watton, J. and D. Seddon, 1994, *Free Markets and Food Riots: The Politics of Global Adjustment,* Blackwell.

World Bank, 1986, *Poverty and Hunger: Issues and Options for Food Security in Developing Countries,* Washington D.C.

World Bank, 1988, *Adjustment Lending: An Evaluation of Ten Years of Experience,* Washington D.C.

World Bank, Poverty and Social Policy Department, 1996, *India's Public Distribution System: A National and International Perspective,* November, Washington D.C.

Index